RECOMMENDATIONS

I have had a front row seat to watch the transformation of Deanna's life, and it has been one of the highlights of my life. As you read her honest and vulnerable story, you will think two things: "The courage and humility of this woman is astounding," and "There is healing, freedom, and hope for everyone."

MIKE BREAUX
Author of *Making Ripples*

Deanna is like family to me. I've lived part of her story and spent plenty of time in darkness as well. I'm so grateful that we both are walking in light these days. Her incredible story will help you see the way there too.

KEITH REPULT
Author of *Just Breathe*

In any discussion of pornography, the focus is nearly always on what harm (if any) it causes the consumer. Very little thought seems to be given to what harm producing pornography can cause. In Purchased: Leaving the Sex Trade, Deanna exposes the raw underbelly of the industry and the heavy toll it exacts on those who appear onscreen. This courageous memoir deserves a wide audience, not just for the harrowing account of her own experience, but also for the note of hope it sounds for those of us who feel beyond the reach of God's grace.

SEAN GLADDING
Author of *The Story of God, the Story of Us and TEN: Words of Hope for an Addicted, Compulsive, Cynical, Divided and Worn-Out Culture*

Despite the global recognition of the #metoo movement, there remains one particular area of society in which survivors' voices are often silenced: the sex industry. Often, we are told that those who perform in pornography or prostitution are empowered, consenting adults who enjoy their work, yet this is often far from reality. With studies revealing that 67 percent of sex industry persons meet the criteria for clinically diagnosed PTSD, stories such as the lived-out experiences of Deanna's are vitally important for others to hear and read.

It takes an enormous amount of courage to reveal not only our triumphs but also the dark, shameful, or embarrassing parts of our lives, something starkly apparent while reading Deanna's story.

Deanna's book tells the tale of a young woman groomed into a life of sexual exploitation and struggling to rise above childhood trauma, self-harm, eating disorders, addiction and abusive relationships But Purchased: Leaving the Sex Trade is ultimately a story of triumph over trauma and discovering the strength to break free and begin thriving. Raw, chilling, empowering, and triumphant, Purchased: Leaving the Sex Trade, has the power to save countless women from walking the path that Deanna once did. This is an absolutely must-read book, particularly for every woman, man, or teen who has been sold the lie that pornography and prostitution are just a job like any other.

JAS RAWLINSON
Mental health speaker, writing coach, and author of
Reasons to Live: One More Day, Every Day'
www.jasrawlinson.com

PURCHASED

LEAVING THE SEX TRADE

DEANNA LYNN

Alpaca Love
PRODUCTIONS

CONTACT INFORMATION / email: purchased4good@gmail.com

PURCHASED: Leaving the Sex Trade
Deanna Lynn

Cover and Internal Design by: John Shaffer @johnshafferart.com

Editing by: Lisa Thompson at www.writebylisa.com. You can email Lisa at writebylisa@gmail.com.

Scripture quotations marked (NIV) are taken from the Holy Bible, New International Version®, NIV®. Copyright © 1973, 1978, 1984, 2011 by Biblica, Inc.™ Used by permission of Zondervan. All rights reserved worldwide. www.zondervan.com The "NIV" and "New International Version" are trademarks registered in the United States Patent and Trademark Office by Biblica, Inc.™

Scripture quotations marked (NASB) are taken from the New American Standard Bible®, Copyright © 1960, 1962, 1963, 1968, 1971, 1972, 1973, 1975, 1977, 1995 by The Lockman Foundation. Used by permission. www.Lockman.org

Some names have been changed to protect the identity of those individuals.

Disclaimer: This book contains mature content and possible triggers. It is intended for a mature audience only. Please use discretion when reading this book.

The events as portrayed herein represent the author's perspective of what happened.

ISBN: 9781697556858

To every person
in my tribe who has
pointed me to the path
that leads to life.

TABLE OF CONTENTS

FOREWORD

Refuge for Women was started with the goal of providing a safe place for women to seek healing and find refuge. I didn't know at the time of launching this ministry just how far people would travel to find this kind of place or experience the kind of transformation that I have witnessed. I knew it needed to be a place where women could have plenty of time to share the traumas they had suffered and learn to dream again of what life could be like if they were pursuing what they wanted instead of what has been a result of force or unresolved pain.

You will find a story of redemption in this book. Deanna willingly opens up and shares her journey so others can see and experience what happens when a woman encounters some of the darkest places on Earth. The good news is that she did not stay in those places but chose a new path and added chapters to her story as a transformed individual. Her story is filled with hope and new beginnings.

Deanna graduated from Refuge for Women in 2012. and often shares about her experience in the program. She was determined to face her pain and find freedom on the other side and today, is a brand new individual. She came to Kentucky with the attitude that this was a life or death situation, and she needed this awareness for the program to work. The good news is that it did work, and we could not be more proud.

This book will help create an accurate picture of the harsh realities of sex work. When I talk to groups around the country, I frankly tell them that many women in the clubs and on screens don't love the work they are doing. I tell them these are real women who have experienced a lot of tragedy that led to their present situation. We currently have six houses filled with women with similar traumas. As you read Deanna's story, I hope that you see a real individual. She rose to places the world may say are successful, but deep down, Deanna was longing for so much more.

When Deanna married her husband, Matt, a few years ago, I saw a new chapter unfolding in a couple that wanted to give their lives to serve others. They completed the necessary academic requirements and have started this new season of service. It has been an honor to have a front row seat to this couple's journey and to play a small role investing into their lives.

Deanna has graciously shared her story with you—the reality of a woman's life before and after being sold. For the sake of forty to forty-two million women who are still selling themselves today in the sex trade, I hope that all of us will commit to help reduce the demand for sexual services around our country and the world. Women's lives are at stake!

Together!
KED FRANK
President of Refuge for Women

Refuge for Women is a non-profit, faith based organization providing specialized long-term care for women who have escaped human trafficking or sexual exploitation. With multiple locations across the U.S., Refuge for Women offers up to twelve months of safe housing, at no charge to the resident, with around the clock care as clients progress through evidence-based, trauma-informed programming. The compassionate staff is trained to help residents work through the program to reclaim their identities and reach their goals to overcome addictions, heal from trauma and develop life skills leading to healthy, balanced living and financial independence. Refuge for Women strives to help each woman complete the program with a vision for her future, equipped to succeed and sustain a life marked with dignity and hope.

INTRODUCTION

We live in a culture increasingly influenced by porn. Sex is used to sell everything, from household products to cars to electronics. Provocative and popular fiction like 50 Shades of Gray is encouraging people to play with a fire that could destroy their homes. We supposedly stand against sex trafficking, and then we turn around and increase the demand through our music, clothing, and movie choices. These decisions to entertain ourselves with increasing shock factor reveal that most audiences are currently numb to the publicizing and proliferation of what was once deemed private.

Amidst this sex-satiated culture, I want to give a realistic view of the life of someone who once allowed herself to be sold. In sharing my own story and journey into and out of the sex industry, I want to educate others in a way that encourages us to stop buying sex in all forms and instead to honor one another as whole people. I want to encourage us to consider the woman who has been made a sex symbol so that we learn to honor both who she was before and who she might become if given an opportunity to succeed in a life outside of selling her body. I have encountered many men and women who were put into this life by their pimps and boyfriends. Others entered it while trying to escape their own trauma and trying to gain some control or dignity in their own lives. Yet others truly believe they can do nothing else. I want to offer you a glimpse of the mentality of a young girl who thought this was her best option in life.

As a woman who was once purchased, I am often placed into one of two categories: I am either victimized as a survivor of human trafficking, or my trauma is dismissed since I chose to enter the commercial sex industry. This is an unhelpful and extreme distinction—especially when some of those fighting to end trafficking are also those who justify their use of pornography, brothels, strip clubs, and escort services because they believe all these women choose to be there. Choice is not always a simple matter when it is derived from decades of compounding trauma, addictions, and lack of quality guidance. For this reason, I want to show you what life looks like when a person says yes to being sold.

This book is not meant to leave readers in despair but rather to depict enough of my own journey through deception to invite appreciation of the freedom possible with complete surrender. I want to show how hope gives birth to new life, when a true chance to heal and opportunities to flourish are given. No one is too far gone. However, no one can complete the journey in isolation.

In this sense, I hope my story can also aid those who want to mentor other women on their journeys of healing and redemption. My desire is that the full presentation of my background—and the way it fed into my choices—can help offer understanding about the many layers of hurt that are present for women leaving the sex industry. More than the woman's body has been wounded, and many memories that stretch much further back than her start in the industry will need to be opened up and healed. Freedom does take work. But it is an infinitely good and worthwhile work.

I personally engaged in my deepest healing efforts at the Refuge for Women in Kentucky. And there, I discovered a place to be truly safe for the first time in my life. I remember lying in my bed each night and saying to myself, "I am safe. I am loved. I am secure." Because of the hard work I did there, I can still say and mean those words today, many years later. If you are called to help a woman walk this road, please let my story invite you into awareness of the layers involved in both her hurt and her healing. And whether you read this story as a mentor or a mentee, let it encourage you of the good and the freedom yet in store.

Ultimately, I hold to the unshakable belief that there here is hope and help for everyone. I hope my story confirms this for you.

CHAPTER ONE

SEEKING ESCAPE

THE EIGHT-YEAR OLD GIRL burst into Christopher's house.

"Whoa, there! What's your rush?"

Gasping for air, she took the glass of water Christopher's dad offered her. Tears streamed down her cheeks. "Can I *please* live with you from now on? I don't want to go home."

"Christopher, take her to your room and get ready for skating. I'll talk to mom and see what we can figure out."

Smiling, the girl was sure she had convinced his parents of her need for rescue. *They'll probably even adopt me,* she thought.

She lay in Christopher's bed. The hem of her stretched-out sweater rose up against her thigh as it twisted in the sheets. She'd adjusted this sweater as a mini-dress, channeling Julia Roberts of *Pretty Woman*. She would offer herself to any boy at the skating rink who'd take her in so she could make her own way out of this life she lived. As she planned her escape, her courage grew within her chest like a bird mounting on its wings and taking flight. Her small hands curved into fists, clenched in determination beneath the sheets. *Everything will work out! I just know it!*

But abrupt and heavy-handed pounding echoed through the room, suddenly pulling her from her own thoughts.

"Knock, knock, knock!"

Her breath caught in her throat. Could the wood on the door feel the anger bursting through that fist? *She* could feel it on the other side of the door. The heart that had soared only moments before took a dive into her now-churning stomach as her dad's voice bellowed through the door.

Oh no, was her single, sinking, desperate thought. He swept into the room, and the sting of embarrassment—or was it terror?—crept across her cheeks. How could he have found her here? And in a boy's bed! She was so sure she'd never be found again . . . never be missed . . . finally be free. But she *was* **found, and she** *wasn't* **free.**

That little girl was me.

My dad hurried me into the car. "Do you know how worried mom and I have been?" He tugged at my short tufts of hair. "And what have you done? What will mom say about your hair?"

I had no idea what to say, so I got in the car. My mother took meticulous care of both my and my sister's beautiful long blonde hair. Earlier that day, I had chopped it off to my shoulders—the hair that my mom was unusually proud of—using a pair of plastic school scissors in the school bathroom. For some reason—and this has stuck with me throughout my life—I assumed that if my hair was different, I would be unrecognizable. I could turn into anybody I wanted with the right hair color and length.

I walked into the house, holding my breath. My mom reacted exactly as I'd feared and as I'd hoped. I'd finally gotten her attention.

"Your hairrrr!" she screamed. "If you wanted to cut it yourself, why couldn't you at least make it even? Well, I'll fix that this instant!"

She grabbed me and pulled me into the bathroom. Yanking my hair, she began snipping. The scissors grazed the skin of my neck. I squinted my eyes, the tears streaming down my face, afraid to look at what she was doing.

"Open your eyes! I hope you're happy. There. If you wanted your hair cut, that's what you got. Exactly what you deserved. How do you like it *now*?" Her words hissed in anger as she tugged at me once more for good measure.

Trembling, I dared to peek my eyes open. I looked at my reflection in shame. I met her eyes, which were filled with disgust, in the mirror. My formerly waist-long hair was now an inch long all over my entire head.

Minutes later, I took my position next to the giant container of birdseed in the Arizona room. We always had huge containers of food available for all the stray birds my mom liked to bring home. She raised them in this room that we had turned into an aviary. I looked down at the poop-covered floor that I spent my time cleaning on my hands and knees for hours every couple of days. My mom didn't use a mop growing up, and if that was good enough for her, it should be good enough for me. I did have a putty knife to scrape the bird droppings off the tile—the hard, dried poop that scraped my knees. The tiny scratches absorbed the Pine Sol, leaving my skin burning on the floor. This was one of many chores I did to satisfy her obsessive cleaning standards.

But this time, I wasn't in the room for chores. I was bent over the trash barrel of wild birdseed with my pants down. My dad's belt was off, and my bottom was whipped because I had tried to run away. The more I cried, the more lashes I got.

My mom yelled for me from the bathroom. I walked through the living room as a movie played on the wooden-framed Curtis Mathes TV. The screen displayed the image of a bathtub filled with rose petals. I didn't know the name of the movie, but interestingly enough, I could smell the roses on TV! No, wait. That was the gallons of rose-scented bubble bath my mom used in the tub. She called me into the bathroom, which was usually where I spent some of my favorite moments with her. My sister and I loved to sit on the toilet and talk to her as she took a bath. I headed through the hallway. Maybe my punishment was over, and she wanted to reassure me that she loved me.

But when I walked in the bathroom, blood-stained towels were scattered across the floor. The pink Daisy disposable razors had become her weapons of choice yet again. My crying mom yelled, "Look at what you're doing to me, you little b*$@&!" I ran out screaming, only to see the expressions of disappointment on my dad's and sister's faces. Disappointment in me for doing this to my mother.

I grabbed the phone to call 911.

"No!" Dad yelled.

We need help. Mom needs help. Why would we not *call 911?* I wondered. But deep inside, I already knew. Because then someone might find out about the ongoing insanity in our home. We knew the routine: Do whatever it takes to make Mom happy and throw away the razors and the blood-stained towels.

.... ◇ ....

We knew the routine. Do whatever it takes to make Mom happy and throw away the razors and the blood-stained towels.

.... ◇ ....

We cleaned up her mess, and as usual, she went for more wine. *Did she have any wine left? Hadn't she had enough?* I wasn't sure how to fix this.

But Dad tried to stop her. After they yelled and fought about her drinking, my mom threw herself at him. It was time for her to prove she was worth keeping around. How could this virile military man in his twenties resist my mom's sexuality? It didn't matter that the children could hear. It didn't matter that we could sometimes see. When Mom and Dad fought, make-up sex was a must; it was how she felt affirmed. In the backyard, on the living room floor, or in the bedroom next to ours—they were in their own world. To spice things up, they popped an X-rated movie in the VCR and acted out the scenes.

"Deanna, come here. Let's look." My sister opened our bedroom door, her curiosity getting the best of her. What was happening next to the TV? *Oh no!* I would never be able to unsee this. They were using the same movies that Mom sometimes showed me, my sister, and even our friends when dad was away.

A HIJACKED MIND

She had first shown me one of those movies when I was five years old when we lived on a military base in Tucson. My dad was in the Air Force, and my mom—well, I'm not sure what she was doing for work at the time. On that day, the house was strangely quiet. *What's Mom doing? Oh, who cares.* My nose was happily buried in my *Disney Encyclopedia of Health.*

"Deanna, get in here!"

What does she want now? I walked in the room and eighties porn music and moaning blared from the TV. Two people were doing things to each other that I had never seen before. I jumped back and screamed in horror. Sobbing uncontrollably, I ran to my mom to bury my head in her chest.

"Don't be a baby!" she said as she pulled me off herself and turned my head back to the TV to watch what was happening.

"I can't watch this. *Please* don't make me watch this!"

She laughed as she watched my sheer terror. But then she realized she might get in trouble if I told my dad. She turned my head back toward the TV.

"Deanna! Watch. This is how you were made. This is normal. This is life!" From there, she proceeded to explain the birds and the bees to me in graphic detail.

Still crying, I left the room, humiliated, confused, aroused, and nauseated all at the same time. I had no idea what had just happened, but yet I felt ashamed. But I couldn't tell anybody. No one could explain all these emotional and physical reactions to me. I had no idea what they were and what they would lead to. This was only the beginning of how she found ways to torment me. She loved to get a reaction out of me.

She continued to come up with new pranks to humiliate me. A few days later, she surprised me with a new Flintstones T-shirt, a long one that could be worn as pajamas. I was so excited that she thought of me, no matter her motives. Impressed with my enthusiasm as I tried it on, she begged me to go show my dad. I raced into the living room. Once again, my heart plunged. My dad was sitting nude on the couch, obviously ready for my mom to join him. I started screaming and turned around. She laughed and told me it was okay and turned me right back around to face my dad. He grabbed a pillow to cover himself up. What else could he do? He shook his head in disbelief but said nothing in an effort to avoid a fight.

As a young child, my mom forced me to watch every horror movie that she liked. I tried my best to act like a grown-up when we watched *Nightmare on Elm Street*, *Puppet Masters*, *Child's Play*, Stephen King movies, and the rest of the R-rated tapes she had in her illegally dubbed collection. I distinctly remember the movie *Carrie*, because at the end, her hand popped up out of the grave. Every time this scene played, my mom jumped at me and scared me even more. She promised that she wouldn't do it each time, saying, "Keep your eyes on the screen." *Bam!* And then she'd laugh hysterically in perverse delight as she watched me, her little girl, cry in terror. This was the woman who was supposed to make me feel safe. I felt anything but.

On top of the abuse and trauma, any remaining sense of safety left when my parents brought my sister and me to a large room with a big table and a counselor. They sat us down and told us that the man raising us was not our biological father. That moment, combined with the other abuse and trauma in our home, shattered any ability I had to cope as a child and manifested in further behavioral disorders. My parents took me to a doctor in search of help to control my behaviors. The doctor initially diagnosed me with Attention Deficit Hyperactive Disorder (ADHD). The doctor didn't know any of the atrocities I was witnessing at home, so with his advice, they sent me off to a psychiatric institution. I don't remember exactly when I entered or how long I stayed. I do know that I started taking various pills prescribed by multiple psychiatric doctors—medications they kept adjusting and increasing for the next fifteen years.

My parents continued living on the base with my sister while I, a preschooler, was staying in the mental institution. By day, I was doing classwork, and by night, all supervision vanished. I had confusing interactions with older residents although the details are not clear. Even so, I felt safer at the facility than at home, so I enjoyed living there. (This facility has since closed.) Every time we behaved well and completed our homework, we got to pick a prize from the closet. I liked reaching goals as it made me feel empowered. When I achieved these goals, my mother approved of me and was happy I was her daughter.

By Easter, my behavior was good enough to earn a pass home. That morning, I hopped out of bed. I could already imagine the smell of the rose bushes outside my house. Once I arrived, I began celebrating with my family.

But in no time at all, my sister and I were bickering. "Stop it!" I yelled as my sister began taunting me to get a rise out of me. "I saaaaid, stop it!" I took matters into my own hands the only way I knew how. I picked up the biggest pink plastic Easter egg I could find and threw it at her. *Pow*! I looked up. My mom's face was riddled with disappointment.

Of course, Mom and Dad would walk outside right now. Right when the Easter egg hit my sister.

They immediately packed up my stuff and drove me back to the institution. As if it weren't bad enough that my visit was cut short, they made sure to tell the counselors about my latest outburst. I had to put back my most recent prize, and I was sentenced to a longer stay at the facility. I was punished and isolated from my family for acting like a typical five-year-old and throwing a toy at my nine-year-old sister. I thought, *I must really be a burden to this family if they keep sending me back here. They just don't want me around.*

I managed to stay the course, finish up my program, and was released to my family and my new school. Halfway through my kindergarten year, Mom and Dad told my sister and me that we were moving off the base. After many work trips away and coming home to his drunk wife, Dad had a decision to make. He would take us with him to Germany or leave the military. He decided that moving to Germany was not the best plan for us as a family at this time. Maybe leaving the military was the fresh start we all needed. And maybe, if Mom had a job, she wouldn't drink so much. So she became an insurance agent, which became her new obsession.

In addition to obsession with work and addiction, sick cycles of codependency were being solidified before my eyes, and not only between my dad and her. One night after we moved, she was so furious she punched him in the stomach, grabbed my sister, and took off. My thirteen-year-old sister didn't know what to do, afraid that if she didn't step over Dad to go with Mom, she would never see Mom again. As her oldest daughter and as her friend, she would always be by Mom's side. I peered out from the blinds of the new Arizona room window as Mom's maroon Nissan Stanza peeled out of the driveway with my sister in the passenger seat. This was one of the many times Mom was ready to leave me behind. Dad was always taking whatever abuse Mom dished out. Now she was never home, and when she was, she was working and still drinking.

I started my new school as a kindergartener and made friends with my neighbors. They played hide-and-go seek at the hotel down the street with my sister and me. It was hot, but my mom did not trust us with a key to the house. We had to play at the hotel or wait outside in the desert heat until our parents came home.

After spending the summer with our neighbors and enjoying the start to our new school year, we ventured back to the hotel to get free maraschino cherries from the bar and ride the elevators. As we chased each other from floor to floor, we came across porn magazines in the trash. *This is awesome!* I thought. *This is just like what my mom shows me.* We were excited and wanted to look for more magazines. My fifth-grade sister and I already knew all about this game. We decided to take it up a notch and invite these neighbors, ages six and ten, to our house. (We had finally figured out how to unlock the latch to the house from the Arizona room.) The four of us took turns practicing stripping for each other while the other two of us peeped through the bathroom window.

We thought this was wildly fun and tried to figure out what we could next. My sister found the Polaroid camera, and she and the other girl positioned me and the younger boy to make our own porn. Of course, at that age, nothing much happened. That time. We continued this behavior with each other all year.

A few days later, the neighbor girl and I were alone. She took it upon herself to teach me how to kiss. She went with me in the house, and we grabbed one of my parent's special adult movies. We each took turns doing everything the movie showed us in the same spot where I had seen my parents' live reenactment. My mom embarrassed me in many ways, including telling me that my biological father was gay and that it was hereditary. This experience sealed the deal. At seven years old, I concluded that I must be a lesbian.

I knew next to nothing about human sexuality except what porn had taught me. I didn't know how to tell anyone that I had sex and might not be a virgin anymore. I was so confused about what happened with the neighbor children that I went to school and told everyone that I was pregnant. I even had a baby shower on the playground of my elementary school. I said I was raped by a fifth-grade boy I had a crush on. This lie continued until I made up a fake name to clear him because I didn't want to tell everyone that a girl "got me pregnant."

My fight continued to gain the attention I was not getting at home, and I started to seek out more sexual behaviors to self-soothe. Although I was a little girl, I began having sexual dreams and woke up both aroused and embarrassed. I started sneaking into the house to watch all the illegally recorded movies we had, and I fast-forwarded to the parts that caused that same physical stimulation in me that happened in my sleep. My mom wouldn't allow me to watch these scenes in normal movies but had no problem showing them to me in the X-rated videos. At the same time, I started using my Barbie dolls to act out the perverse things I saw my parents do on the living room floor. As a first grader, I envisioned how badly I wanted to be a porn star during my mile-long walk to school. Maybe that would be how I made it in the world. Maybe that would arrest the addiction that had already begun.

TAKING MATTERS INTO MY OWN HANDS

Child Protective Services came to visit us twice in Tucson, and both visits occurred much later, after I was first shown the films at the military base. The first visit happened after my sister's friend's parents found out about my mom's daytime X- rated viewings with us. The second time they came was because I showed my friends my bruises at school—bruises I intentionally made bigger in the school bathroom so somebody would get us help. Both times, CPS confiscated the movies. More movies always appeared after CPS left and throughout my entire childhood.

I didn't understand why pornography kept coming into our lives. I did not realize that it was already starting to shape who I was. Exposure to live sex and porn was influencing how I viewed others and myself.

It wasn't only porn that was affecting my view of sex. Every day, mainstream movies made selling sex look glamourous. My mom had a fascination with the movie *Pretty Woman*. As she drank her boxes of wine in the middle of the night, she popped in her fairy-tale romance of a prostitute who found love. Once in a while, when she grew lonely and depressed, she woke up either my sister or me to watch it with her. If we were lucky, we got to sip orange soda and eat bonbons. We were too young to recognize the emotional incest that was occurring as my mom's only friends besides her husband. My sister and I simply felt special when we were needed by our mom to join her in glamorizing this story line. This story gave me the idea to dress myself as an eight-year old prostitute and run away, ready to do anything as long as I didn't have to go home. In addition, the porn movies I had watched made me think I could use my sexuality in hopes a boy would hide me from my family forever.

> ············· ◇ ·············
>
> *It wasn't just porn*
>
> *that was affecting*
>
> *my view of sex. Every day,*
>
> *mainstream movies*
>
> *made selling sex*
>
> *look glamourous.*
>
> ············· ◇ ·············

My escape did not end up like Julia Roberts's character. Not this time or when I grew up and lived out the actual story in greater detail minus the human savior. I was back where I felt unwanted, and Mom once again put the attention back on herself after another supposed suicide attempt. We all went back to pretending as if everything were fine in our house.

CHAPTER TWO

OUR NEW NORMAL

"DEANNA! DEANNA! Wake up!" my sister frantically yelled. I was vividly dreaming of beautiful white polar bears swimming around, and yet she had the nerve to shake me into consciousness. "Something has happened to Mom!"

Suddenly I was wide awake. *Did Mom run away again? Drive off drunk? Attempt suicide?* My sister raced with me to Mom's bedroom. At my left, my mom was on the floor next to her bed. Dad was crying over her. I started screaming. "What did Dad do to Mom?"

Sirens echoed down the street. Mom was unconscious, being carried out on a stretcher. We went over to the neighbor's house and watched out their living room curtains as the ambulance took off. Mom had had a massive heart attack, an anomaly with no apparent cause, according to the doctors.

She remained unconscious in the hospital for her entire stay, and we visited her regularly. My sister went off to Germany to fulfill her summer foreign-exchange program before starting high school. I went about life, incorporating my mom's new condition into my routine. At the hospital, I sat by her bed, talking to her and telling her how we would celebrate my upcoming birthday there if we had to. I had just finished fourth grade and was sure my mom would see me to fifth.

My sister returned from Germany on a typical hot desert summer day in August and went to the hospital to see my mom. The next day, on August 10, 1994, we had appointments: my sister at the dermatologist, and I at the eye doctor. We planned to go to the hospital to visit mom.

Finally, someone could prove that I really couldn't see. Before my mom's heart attack, she refused to believe I needed glasses, and dad stood up for me and fought with her. She then withdrew her approval and love for us. By now, I had already become a habitual liar, so she might have had her reasons to doubt me. I made up extreme stories to get attention from her or anyone. At school, I told everyone I was blind. My classmate Stuart did not buy it and kicked me on the playground to see if I would flinch. Smart—mean, but smart. But here I was, two years later, and I was almost legally blind. Time for glasses.

The coming inevitable sneers of my classmates didn't matter because if these glasses helped me resemble my mother, I thought, then maybe . . . just maybe, it would bring me closer to her.

I picked out a pair of plastic frames constructed of two thick, giant beige squares. They looked exactly like my mom's and covered nearly my entire face. I was practically begging to be laughed at. My head was bigger than most of my tiny body. Kids at school called me "shrimp" and "bug eyes." Now, the lenses magnified my already-giant blue eyes—the eyes Mom used to say she got on Blue Light Special at Kmart. (She was covering up my different physical appearance since people could tell I was adopted. I had inherited my eyes from my biological father.) The coming inevitable sneers of my classmates didn't matter because if these glasses helped me resemble my mother, I thought, then maybe, just maybe, it would bring me closer to her.

I got into the car with my dad, now the proud new owner of glasses that looked like mom's. At first, I missed the heaviness in the air around us. I gave little thought to the silence between us as we drove to retrieve my sister from her mole-removal appointment. My mind was busy painting hopeful images of the pleasure that would cross Mom's face at the sight of my new frames. But then as my sister got in the car and we started to head back home, I was suddenly pulled from my musings as I watched different scenery pass by my window.

Wait. This isn't the direction of the hospital, I thought. Confused and mildly concerned, I remained silent. I didn't want to question my weary father, who was already juggling so much. Swallowing hard, I shifted my gaze to study his face. I watched him in the rearview mirror, tracing his familiar features in my mind. The strange strain around his eyes was recent. He shifted uncomfortably in the driver's seat, and my stomach performed a tiny flip. I suddenly felt too warm. The knot in Dad's throat was getting bigger and . . . louder. The strangled sounds of his own failed attempt at composure broke the deafening silence. He would never react with the same intense heartbroken weeping that he did this day.

His words broke the silence and my whole world in the same moment. "Girls, Mommy won't be coming home." He exerted immense effort to remain calm. "She's gone."

The horrible words hung in the air of the Mazda, like suspended shards of glass frozen in time. "Gone," echoed through my mind, skittering around and ramming hard into the edges of my consciousness. A deep ache spread like a plague across my chest. "She's gone." *And oh, how the words took their time, stabbing me slowly, while I sank into the hollow truth of my new reality.*

I started banging my head against the back of my sister's car seat. What do I do with this information? Just the other day, I heard her cough. I thought that meant she was getting better! Is that why they rushed me out of the room? I naively believed that one noise meant she was coming back to us. Dad said if Mom had ever regained consciousness, she would have been a vegetable. She would not have wanted that.

When I saw her in the casket, she was gone. Completely gone. Not only was her makeup poorly done, but she looked nothing like her beautiful self. Her soul, the light that shone through her, was no longer with us. The only other funeral I had attended was for my grandpa. He had looked so lifeless in his casket too. No amount of makeup for him or for my mother could bring them back. Nothing could realistically portray the beauty my mom had from the energy and heart she carried on her good days.

Good days looked like the day she got off work early and surprised me by picking me up from the after-school program. She planted a bright red kiss on my cheek to embarrass me in front of my classmates, but I welcomed the affection and did not hesitate to leave her lipstick mark there. Another day, she had me sing REM's "Losing My Religion" in the middle of Target to the employees, and they went to find the CD it was on. She also used this tactic when CPS came; I sang songs from *The Little Mermaid* and acted as if I was a normal little girl. She tried to distract CPS from what was really going on in our home. These were yet more performances from my mom, but they are the closest things I have to good memories of her.

In any case, that was all gone now. I wrote a song for her funeral, the last song I would sing in her presence. In one final goodbye, I touched her face that felt like cold hard jelly. My mom was no longer with her body. She was free. Free from all she was trying to manage, mask, or run from. Free from sickness, alcoholism, and depression. Free to be the soul she was created to be.

LIFE WITHOUT MOM

Three weeks later, my sister entered her freshman year of high school, and I went into fifth grade. We both were always striving to be the best like my mom would have wanted. My intelligent sister was placed in the best university-prep high school Tucson had to offer, and she was a cheerleader for the wrestling team. But internally, she, too, was struggling.

I, however, was wrestling the boys and thoughts thereof. Similar to how boys sometimes pull girls' pigtails when they develop a crush, I liked to throw guys down by their shirts and trip them. I never wanted to fight girls; I just wanted to prove myself to the guys. Like my sister, I was also intelligent, but I was a troublemaker. My report cards said, "Deanna is a bright student, but she is too disruptive." Because of my ADHD, I could not sit still. I was anxious and could not focus. It was time to up the medications again and go back to counseling.

The popular girls in fifth grade were already dating and seeing how far they could get with the boys our age. They let me hang out with them but made sure I knew my place. They made fun of me and continually tore me down, reminding me they were cooler than me. They told me in front of everyone that I had killed my mother. I swallowed the pain of that statement, right there under the ramada, and I wondered, *Could they be right*? After all, my mother had told me I was the reason she no longer wanted to live. I stuck with these so-called friends anyway, figuring that when they were done with whoever was cool, I would be next to be affirmed. I was never picked first for anything, but hey, at least I was invited.

Most of my friends' parents were divorced, and others had a deceased parent, so none of us had a healthy example of what a functional family looked like. We thought gang life looked appealing, so we began to imitate what they did. In our neighborhood, people had the choice of representing two different gangs. Even though my friends at this age were not officially jumped in, we were all quick to claim membership to something in order to belong. Most of us had siblings, cousins, family, or boyfriends who were in the gangs, so each person had backup on hand—even at ten years old—if someone wanted to start a fight. At my school, everyone had something to prove.

One of these friends, Gina, invited me to my first sleepover. I liked her. She fought her own fights. I had never been allowed to go to sleepovers before, and I definitely wanted this to be my first one. My sister, however, was encouraged to have sleepovers, and Mom bought them fun things to do and eat. I sometimes got to play by myself with some of their toys, such as new board games, workbooks, and my favorite, Sand by Numbers. While my sister played with friends, I amused myself with games and read through dictionaries and the elegant gold-trimmed and embossed-maroon hardcover *World Book Encyclopedias*. Their smooth, shiny illustrated pages of whatever I wanted to know delighted the mind, eyes, and hands, and they smelled like they were fresh off a press.

My mom wasn't around to say "no," and my sister told my dad I was ready. My first sleepover was nothing like my sister's. No parents seemed to be around, and if they were, they were likely stoned on marijuana. Since Gina had a twin brother who also invited friends, this sleepover was co-ed. We played make-out games like Spin the Bottle and 7 Minutes in the Closet. Again, I was never picked, and with each rejection, my self-worth slipped further and further away.

At midnight, they pulled out the Ouija board to contact their dead relatives. Since my mom had recently passed, I knew I would not be left out of this game. I did anything to feel that I belonged, even contacting the deceased. We started to call on them for help. I had no idea what I was opening myself up to. I don't know what I was looking for, but I was willing to invite any spirit in just to make me feel . . . feel something—anything.

At only eleven, we had lived with more internal pain than any human could bear. We were remorseful, sorrowful, lonely, tired, and desperate for a better life.

SPIRITUAL BEGINNINGS

I had no spiritual foundation. My family and friends were all searching for healing, truth, and affirmation in their own ways. Even though I didn't yet know it, God had already made a way for me. I learned more about that at a concert shortly after my first sleepover.

The same group of friends that attended the sleepover invited me to a Christian rap concert. At the time, we were all into Bone Thugs-N-Harmony, Snoop Dogg, and all sorts of other rappers. We could only imagine how cool a live rap concert would be.

Little did we know, we were about to be emotionally wrecked. Somehow, by the end of the night, all of us knew that the life we were living was pointless and that we ourselves were hopeless if left on our own. At only eleven, we had lived with more internal pain than any human could bear. We were remorseful, sorrowful, lonely, tired, and desperate for a better life. That was a starting point for us, because in that moment, I believe we all invited Christ into our hearts to help guide us back to a right relationship with God. A relationship we had a part in but could not restore ourselves.

We thought our lives would be different after that concert. Maybe we wouldn't have to live like we used to. We were ready to live in this new-found freedom. But as the concert ended, so did our feelings about what had happened. Like the others, I only knew one way to live. No one was around to demonstrate this godly life or to help us pursue it. We were left to continue seeking and searching in the only ways we knew how, and for me, that meant resorting to witchcraft. I needed to feel connected to a higher power and to my mom, so I went back to the Ouija board.

My involvement with the Ouija board continued into middle school. Around the same time, the movie *The Craft* came out. It motivated me to find more friends with an interest in witchcraft. I performed money spells, and instead of raining money, I was given opportunities to steal. Stealing, involvement in witchcraft, horoscopes, and burning incense to influence outcomes—this was the road I chose to lead me to my future. I was told I had "great energy" and that "witches everywhere were trying to get my gifts." While these were supposed to be compliments, they were instead horrible threats, and I felt as if evil spiritual beings were following me, especially at night. I was attacked in my dreams for countless nights. I had nightmares and night terrors when I could see the ceiling melting and the devil in the corner. I sometimes woke up unable to breathe, feeling as if I were smothered. I became terrified of the dark and sleep and could not figure out why this evil kept chasing me.

I dismissed the obvious signs of the spiritual war I seemed to be in and continued to try to make contact with my dead mother through séances. My friends encouraged me to make blood pacts with them to deepen our bond. With an absent mother and only her earthly example to recall, I began to force love in my own ways. I was casting love spells in an effort to make people love me. I went so far as to carry around a vial of my blood at school in case the opportunity for a new love spell arose. Disappointed with the lack of actual results—and by lack, I mean *no* results—I went back to trying to capture the affection of others the only way I knew how. The way my mom showed me before she died. It was time for me to let go of the dead and all spiritual powers and take back control of my life.

3

TRYING TO FIT IN

I WAS RAGING with hormones in middle school. But my physical body hadn't caught up to the other girls my age. My peers nominated me the poster child for the "teeny-tiny sports bra committee." I was in a race against time, a race to grow out of the body of a little girl and start to look like a woman. Or at least a girl my age. Everything was a competition. From school to dating to moving through the bases, everyone did everything quickly while being careful not to get caught.

My friends found it entertaining to move me to the next level, so they set me up with my first boyfriend. We were both petite with blond hair and blue eyes. Though Brett was kind and a great guy, he was merely a way to advance me toward my initiation into the preteen years. I was generally only interested in the boys my friends were interested in. These were tough guys who got in fights and usually dressed like thugs. That was definitely not Brett, but he was the first guy willing to make out with me, so I took advantage of the opportunity.

We put together a plan to make out. It was technically the first time for both of us—well, since I had reenacted my mom's porn movies with a girl, but those memories were deeply buried by now. We found a quiet spot on the steps, and my friends spread the word around school so that witnesses could arrive in time for the show. He strolled toward me. *Here he comes,* I thought. *I guess this is it. If I wrap my tongue with my bubble gum, will it be less gross?* Either way, everyone else was doing it, and this was my time to shine. Out came the disposable cameras, flashing away. My first romantic kiss was about to become the first of many intimate moments displayed publicly and on film. *Okay, we got that over with,* I thought with a sigh of relief. *I guess it's time to hold hands now.*

GETTING HIGH

That courtship did not last long. Those butterflies some people get when venturing into a new relationship were enough to nauseate me. I got the validation I needed; the relationship was only a show. Unfortunately, Brett honestly liked me, but I didn't know what to do when somebody showed legitimate interest. The whole façade was making me sick. I didn't like him; I didn't know what it was like to be liked for myself.

I definitely wanted to be cool, and I thought I needed a boyfriend to do that. After all, everyone else seemed to have one. But I didn't feel cool; I felt like an imposter. I began to revert back to my childhood habit of treating boys (him) roughly, thinking that maybe if I pushed him around enough, he would finally dump me. Yes, I would be the meanest person possible in the relationship, and then maybe he would leave. After all, surely it was in his best interest. This pattern of behavior worked for me, just like it had for my mom, so I continued it throughout school and my early adult years.

Though I learned to use people for attention, when I was used and thrown away by guys, I was devastated. Whenever one of the cool guys paid attention to me, they broke up with me for one of my friends, just like at my last school. The constant rejection hurt so badly, I'd beat myself up physically in an effort to control my own pain. One way I released the anguish was by pounding my head against the lockers or banging it on cement. I hit my head hard enough to hurt but not hard enough to split it open—because I had already done that in elementary school, trying to show off with a cartwheel that landed me right into a brick wall. It was horribly bloody, and as if the pain weren't enough, my mom took out her fury on me because she had to leave work and take care of my mess.

No mess this time, only enough external pain to express my internal hurts.

I also developed another less obvious way to harm myself. Starving. *Maybe if I don't eat*, I thought, *someone will notice, reach out, and try to care for me.* My stomach was in knots from distress, which helped suppress my appetite. This tactic worked as a temporary numbing strategy. After a certain point, I became so high from the self-punishing and the lack of food, I forgot the pain that originally catapulted me into the self-destructive behavior. My sickly looking outsides began to match how I felt inside.

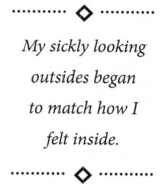

My sickly looking outsides began to match how I felt inside.

I was doing the best I could and trying to cope in my own strength and self-control. But that wasn't cutting it. Then, I discovered pot, thanks to my friend Reese—who, interestingly enough, also brought me to church after-school programs on nights we didn't feel like going home. She taught me how to memorize verses, hide drugs in my makeup, and make pipes out of aluminum foil or Altoid tins. Instead of walking home after school, we'd walk to Ali's house.

I previously tried to date Ali, a sweet guy, in an effort to keep up with my maturing friends. His mom took us on a pizza date and then left us alone in his room to make out. I broke up with him shortly after that when he got too close emotionally. After our break up, he was now ready to experiment with drugs. Since we brought the drugs, he and his friend welcomed us as his guests.

Four of us agreed to go for it. "Puff, puff, pass," they said. The words played on repeat in my mind, and I prepared myself to perform the deed. My heart beat in time with the mantra: Puff (*thump-thump*) . . . puff (*thump-thump*) . . . pass (*thump-thump*)—repeat.

It was my turn, and a mild curiosity mingled with a dull ache inside me. I held the joint and took my time following the instructions, which were still looping, a silent echo in my head. Smoke filled my senses, and I closed my eyes when they watered. A hard elbow shoved into my side, and my eyes jerked back open.

"Hey, pass that to me."

Whatever. I didn't care if they thought they had waited too long. I had no plans to do this again, so I was making the most of the moment. But even these thoughts were already becoming fuzzy around the edges. Images wreathed in vibrating waves of sickening motion swirled through my mind.

"I feel fine, guys. This stuff isn't affecting me one bit," I said, surprisingly aware that I was watching myself become high. Like an all-seeing eye suspended above my body, I was, for the moment, detached and deadened to the sensations even now flowing through my blood and brain.

Ali finished his turn. I reached my fingers toward his face, slightly misjudging the angle. I brought them back toward me; only I forgot the pass. "I need a few more hits," I said, dodging an attempt from his friend to take it away. "I'll give it back in a minute." As I spoke, a thought suspended before me. *I don't know if I'll be able to give this up.*

But then that fleeting bit of fear sank into shadow as an overpowering, much more immediate sensation kicked in. A sudden onset of cravings flooded my brain. With no regard as to where I was, I ransacked the cabinets, shoving aside boxes of tasteless cereal and unappealing canned foods. Barely able to control myself, I was on a mission to acquire a very particular reward: goldfish crackers.

"Deanna has the munchies," Ali taunted, laughing at me until the others joined him. The resulting paranoia kicked in. My jumbled thoughts fought with each other for prominence. *Am I chewing with my mouth open? Did I swallow? Am I going to die choking on goldfish crackers? Why is my mouth so dry? I think I hear Ali's parents. What am I going to do?*

I used every ounce of strength to stand up against what felt like a force field around me. "You guys, this isn't funny. I feel trapped. Get me out of this invisible bubble!" I began to panic. Tears threatened as a lumped lodged at the back of my throat. My voice sounded increasingly unfamiliar. What *was* that voice?

"Is that *my mom*? Do you hear her? Mom! Mom!" My voice rose in pitch as desperation laced the slur of tumbled words. "Mom, where are you? I know you're here!"

The taunting froze, and what had felt like hot, swirling air around me suddenly stood still. Everyone became serious, and someone tried to tell me what I had forgotten in my pot-induced stupor. The strange and hollow words of explanation reached into my internal chaos and deepened the panic. *No*, I thought. *They have to be wrong.* Then as if still outside my body, I heard myself scream. "What do you mean, my mom's dead?" It was as though this were the first time I had heard the news. Unable to process or control my own emotions, I laughed so hard, tears squeezed out. I was hardly aware of the wetness on my cheeks and the fog in my brain. I wailed and then laughed my empty, tortured laugh some more, alternating between mania and despair.

On the walk home, different emotions flooded me. "Ugh, why am I so depressed?" I asked Reese, who had volunteered to walk with me.

"You're coming down," she said. *Thank God!* Being high was the scariest thing I had ever gone through. I hated feeling out of control and delusional.

We went in my house, and I slept it off on the couch. Reese felt moved to write poetry. I didn't have to worry about what Dad would think; he probably wouldn't be home from his second job for hours. Anyway, he usually didn't take out his anger until later at night when he'd go through each room and trash everything out of place. He threw glass, smashed videos, and whipped cords. Once, he even came at me with two by fours. It didn't matter if we had company. He had a point to prove; he was unhappy, tough, in control, and would be heard. But for today, we were safe from his disappointment and lashing out.

WHATEVER IT TAKES

During our last year of middle school, our lives revolved around boys, getting high, and now drinking. We attended the school dance long enough to take a picture with our friends, jump the school fence, and go get drunk at Andy and Jason's house—two cute brothers from school. I was determined that by the end of the night, I'd be making out with one of them. After a few bottles of wine coolers, I was well on my way to accomplishing my goal.

35

Andy and I both loved to drink, and we could care less about the future. He was the carefree guy I was looking for, so I decided to take it slow so that he'd stick around. But a few days later, one of my so-called friends invited him over to her place to hang out with some older girls. She gave him more physically than I was willing to and supplied him with weed. I was heartbroken once again. The girls who *knew* I liked him were so mean and scandalously proved I would never be as popular as they were. And the sting of rejection—oh, the rejection!—cut so deep.

I might not have been popular, but I had one more way to gain respect at this school. It was time to start a fight. In Tucson, it was hard to be a white girl. I was often accused of being a racist, even though I was the one picked on for my race. Classmates were looking for any reason to provoke me into fighting. People thought I was an easy target because I was small. If they said I was racist, then they could justify bullying me. Everyone knew that I hated violence. And yet, I did love to box—not to hurt anyone, but as a sport. I used to have fight practices with friends in my room after school. People were shocked at my forceful punches, and boy, the little person in me loved it when my strength was validated.

I chose two victims and made up drama about them to start a fight. But my plan backfired with the first victim. I called her names in front of the girls I was trying to impress. But those girls teamed up with her instead of siding with me. They gave her all their sharpest rings in hopes of scarring my face. I quickly backed down and had lunch by myself in a classroom instead. It wasn't worth having a permanent reminder of the years I knew I would never want to look back on. I needed a fight big enough to show people I could take care of myself. But I was not willing to risk possible stitches in my face.

The second girl was younger, and I pushed her into the street after getting off the public city bus after school. I followed her again the next day. My stomach did flips at the thought of violence, but I had to find a way to gain the approval of my hardcore peers. Her mom showed up at the bus stop where I was bullying her each afternoon. She was parked down the street, and the second I pushed her daughter, she started honking at me. Ultimately, I was suspended, and the same girls I was trying to impress took victim number two's side as well. They threatened me for messing with her. All I could do at this point was avoid everyone and get home safely until I could figure out a way to get back in their good graces.

Wonder of wonders, I survived middle school without going to the hospital. By the time it was all over, my new plan was to drink the summer away and stick around the people who would agree to be my friends again—at least, long enough to go on the cool camping trips my dad had planned at Lake Patagonia. We would ride jet-skis, eat lots of great food, and hopefully meet some boys with a boat.

We took four-day trips once a month in the summer. My dad took off work, and camping brought out his fun self. My friends all came and crushed on him. They, too, were happy to get away. But this came with ample opportunities for my sister, her friends, and my friends to join in with my cool older sister to make fun of me. Every time I went on a ride on the Wave Runner, they promised not to do anything crazy. But like my mom, who loved to set me up to watch me cry and squirm, they lied, tossed me off, and all laughed as I cried and became angry. Why did everyone find embarrassing me so amusing? I was the only one not having fun in life.

CHAPTER FOUR

HIGH SCHOOL INITIATION

By HIGH SCHOOL, I had now arrived in every way important to me. I had my own lunch money. I could not only fit into a push-up bra, but I could also wear my sister's form-fitting shirts—which made my chest appear bigger than it was. Both of these were signs to me that I was growing up. I was confident this would be my year.

I had plenty of cliques to choose from. My school offered university classes even for freshmen, so I could spend time with my smart friends. I made the cheer squad with other preppie girls. My slacker friends and I sometimes jumped the fence at school, arriving at my house in less than five minutes. Now it was even easier to ditch school and party. My cool older sister officially dropped out of school, became a stripper, got a fake ID, and could get us anything we needed to have a good time. Her gang-banger boyfriends and friends looked out for us in case we needed people who had our backs in times of trouble. I was finally in!

To become more popular, I began to sell weed for some of my sister's boyfriends. One day, some gang members, likely seniors, found out I sold them fake drugs and followed me at lunch. They threatened to beat me with a cane if I didn't give them the drugs I had on me. I did, and as a result, my sister fired me.

It didn't matter; I had plenty of other drugs to do—and when I didn't, I entertained myself with over-the-counter caffeine pills. When they no longer gave me sufficient energy, I turned to the street drugs my sister used, such as crystal meth. Upon coming down, I'd begin drinking in the morning until I'd eventually pass out in a nearby alley in my own green bile. Even after this, I still managed to pull it together by the end of the school day for cheer practice. As a flyer that was thrown in the air, I had to be somewhat conscious. But I *barely* was.

Since I was a junior varsity cheerleader, I began to make friends with the freshman football players. I'd been in school for two months when I saw *him* walking toward me for the first time. He was one of the cutest, most confident guys on the football team, and I happened to be a cheerleader. *What do I need to do to get Mark's attention?* I wondered. I found out he liked to party, so I shared my drugs and alcohol, and in exchange, he paid attention to me. But I knew drugs and making out weren't enough for this man. Before I figured out what my next move would be, the same girl who took home my middle school crush after the dance swooped in to steal his virginity from me. Soon everyone knew. They were the hot topic at school.

They weren't exclusive, though, and I wasn't giving up this time. I initiated make-out sessions with Mark after the games and found ways to smoke pot with him in the stairwells. One day, we decided to take our drug use to another level. A friend brought us roofies, which we later learned were date-rape drugs. He got them from Mexico, where they are known as Mexican Valium. I wanted to show off that I had Mark's attention to everyone, so I sat on his lap in the cafeteria and fed him the pills he had bought from our friend and then took some myself. I don't know how we made it through the rest of the school day. I blacked out until I found myself with him in front of a classroom door with no memory of how I got there. With all my inhibitions gone, I allowed him to take my virginity. People were watching and encouraging us to do it. At the noise of the crowd, my cheerleading coach showed up, yelled, and made us go to practice. *Did I actually lose my virginity?* I wondered. I think both of us were too high to do anything, and I had thought women were supposed to bleed the first time.

I returned home that night, still high out of my mind. I was so high, I was eating a bowl of chili and laughing while staring at my dad instead of the TV. He was furious with me as usual, but I didn't bring up what had happened at school. But he knew that I was high. Usually, he went out drinking or yelled or fought with my sister, blaming her for being a bad influence on me. They always got in screaming matches and fist fights, and my dad broke stuff or disabled her car. Anything to gain some control over our out-of-control lives. But not tonight. Tonight, he merely seemed disappointed with us and with life.

I went back to school the next day, found Mark, and grabbed more pills from the same guy. Round two! Again, I had no recollection of the school day, but I came to in the stairwell with Mark, where fellow students were cheering us on. I was now officially what the girls called me anyway. Then my sister showed up, massive obscenities flying out of her mouth.

"Get off her noooow!"

Crap, I got caught again.

I giggled at the insanity of the moment. Launched into action by my sister's righteous anger, her latest thug boyfriend wasn't messing around. He physically pulled us apart as my sister grabbed my pants that were flung over the stairwell. Even though I was very disoriented, I pulled my shirt down far enough to cover me as I stumbled across the courtyard. Glancing around, not knowing what day or time it was, I wondered why everyone looked so mad.

> *I had no recollection of the school day, but I came to in the stairwell with Mark, where fellow students were cheering us on. I was now officially what the girls called me anyway.*

My sister sobered me up and then let me tag along to a party that night. During the drive, she talked her boyfriend's riled up friends out of hurting Mark. They were furious that a guy would publicly take advantage of me while I was that drugged. After she and the guys sniffed a few lines of cocaine, they calmed down, and she allowed me to join in the fun. I now had pills, weed, alcohol, and cocaine flowing through my blood. I felt like I was flying! And so, consequently, I had found my next drug of choice.

I did a few lines of cocaine and stood to prove to the older crowd that I could hang with the best of them. Only I couldn't seem to leave the bathroom. I became lightheaded, my heart was racing, and sweat was pouring from my face. All the drugs, alcohol, and excitement from the last two days finally caught up with me. My sister raced me to the ER to detox.

I woke up, lying in the hospital, totally freaked out. They planned to pump my stomach . . . until the tests came back. They were negative. *I'm clean?! Why are there no pills in my system? Did I throw up everything? Did the pills cancel each other out? Do I even know what drugs I took?* They found no trace of anything. *Great, now everyone thinks I'm a liar.*

MY PRIMARY ADDICTION

When I went back to school, a friend explained to me that I had unknowingly taken date-rape pills. She explained that because I was barely aware of what was happening, I was technically date-raped by Mark and that I should talk to a counselor. I agreed to do so. I told the counselor everything that had happened—and my confession turned the guy who sold us the pills against me. I was now considered a snitch, and he and his friends were looking to take me out, possibly for good. For the next few months, I was afraid to walk home. I was always looking over my shoulder and taking new, longer routes off the beaten path until he moved away.

At the same time, Mark wouldn't talk to me now that rumors were circulating that he had date-raped me. Any time I saw him at a distance, my stomach began to churn, and all the longing and pain I'd built up over my miserably confused life rammed through my chest like a speed train. Oh, how I longed for him to acknowledge me. Oh, how I longed for the floor to open up and swallow me whole. I couldn't have what I wanted, and I couldn't hide from the hurt this created.

That week, we had a school assembly, and the cheer squad performed. I knew all eyes would be on me—and I desperately wanted Mark's gaze to find mine and make everything okay again. By that point, I wasn't concerned with romantic rejection. I wanted him back: his approval, his friendship. As I had given myself to him, he had become my only friend, and I wasn't ready to lose that. So I readied myself to be presentable and powerful and earn my way back to him. I went from barely being conscious, flying in the air a week before, to being completely sober at the top of a cheer stunt, looking out at everyone despite my cowardice.

Hands on my hips, chin tipped toward the sky, I did my best perform well enough to be worthy of attention—trying to hide my fear and my hope and my desperation. Timidity mixed with an aching need for recognition, and my heart pounded in my chest. I tried not to make eye contact with anyone as I scanned the sea of faces. I glanced carefully, slowly, secretly around the room . . . until I finally found him. At that exact moment, my breath caught in my throat—and all my dreams finally died. I couldn't control my intense emotional pain or the resulting physical response, and hot tears began to roll down my cheeks. There he was, in the audience, looking at me with a chilling disdain. Like every last grain of sand slipping through an hour glass, any self-worth I had mustered up for this moment now drained fully away.

This happened week after week at multiple games until I hardened myself sufficiently against the pain and decided to move on—to his friends and teammates. I invited the rest of the football team to my house to continue our drinking charades. I was not about to stay sober. For attention, I started brawls with the big tough guys to show off and went through the rest of the semester seducing whomever and ignoring school all together. Many afternoons, when I should have been in school, my dad found me wandering the streets or drunk and passed out in my waterbed. I glared at him, half-conscious. "What does it matter to you?" I'd challenge him. "You're never home anyway."

I surrendered myself to this party life. I went out all the time with my sister, and sleeping with her friends became a sport for me. I wanted older guys to notice me. Their girlfriends weren't sleeping with them, so I had each of them to myself once the girlfriend went home. The girls eventually found out and threatened me. Still, I did anything possible for validation from others. It was the only time I felt affirmed, as if somebody actually liked me.

Easter weekend, I went out with my own friends from high school to Mark's best friend's house. We had a bottle of Goldschläger. I considered these good, noble friends, and yet they, too, began drinking with us. I was impressed they were holding their alcohol down. After the liquid courage kicked in, I wanted to have all his attention, and I got it. Then we woke up and went to school as if nothing had happened. But by the time I got to campus, my girlfriends were furious. In their jealousy, they told everyone, including me, that I would ruin his reputation.

> *I did anything possible for validation from others. It was the only time I felt affirmed, as if somebody actually liked me.*

One of those girls—my friend Reese, who got me high the first time—found me after class and yelled at me for corrupting him and the other girls at the party. Friends were like family to her, but apparently, I wasn't included in those friends. I was shocked. She was two times my size and was about to use that advantage against me. She ordered me to meet her the next day in the courtyard. I tried to go home without making another scene, but she came running up. In front of everyone, she grabbed me by my shirt, and I grabbed her by hers. "I'm supposed to be your friend," I pleaded with her. "You don't want to do this."

Smack! She slapped me across my face, hoping I would hit her back. We had been friends too long; there was no way I was doing this. She was basically doing to me what I did in middle school in an effort to make her name known on campus. I wouldn't bite. She continued to threaten me and leave me in fear of what was coming next instead of finishing it. She told me this wasn't over and to watch my back. I once again had to look over my shoulders to see who followed me home.

I walked home that day, free for the moment, still caught up in my head and in what had just happened. *I've done everything my mom taught me about using my sexuality as a woman. I've imitated my older sister and other popular girls. But what works for them doesn't work for me. Why?* When I drank, it was too much. When I fooled around, I took it too far. I was controlled by obsessions, addictions, compulsions, and hormones—all too great for me to handle—and I had no one to show me another way. I used everything in my power to fit in, but I ended up being pushed out.

I was done with this school for good. Contrary to the confidence with which I began, I now knew the truth: I was nowhere close to arriving. In fact, it was time for me to leave. My friend, Briana, met me at my house. She had recently switched to an alternative school and thought I would fit in better there. I stood by the front door, crying to my sister about what happened. When my dad came home, she helped me talk my dad into transferring schools. "It isn't safe for her to go back to this school where so many people want to beat her into the ground! Look at her! She needs to start over." My sister was very convincing, so we made the switch. Good-bye, old high school! Hello, new school where I could start over and be myself.

All my broken and confused self.

CHAPTER FIVE

A NOT-SO-FAIRY-TALE ENDING

POOL BALLS SMACKED against each other while I shoveled down French fries covered with nacho cheese to satisfy my hunger. The juke box blared with the usual song, "Smack My Bitch Up." I was at my favorite pool hall with my friend, Briana, who I now attended school with. And by "friend," I mean she was now officially my girlfriend. At least for show, anyway. I wanted love, and she wanted attention. It seemed fitting that I would have a real girlfriend now since my family told me I would be gay. She, however, only wanted to be noticed by the guys. Lesbian make-out sessions were cool, so I let her use me to get the attention she needed. I mainly wanted a close friend, and I thought this might be the way to keep one. However, we only demonstrated our relationship at the pool hall and at parties. It was so entertaining that each of us attracted new college-aged boyfriends.

Pete took me on my first official date. He even picked me up; he had a truck—an older beige and brown truck—but it was ruggedly manly, and it was his. We went to see *American Pie*, not the classiest first date. What I liked most about him was that he communicated what he liked and didn't like in a relationship.

He took me seriously. After a few dates, he took me back to his place where he had a rose garden and an empty guesthouse to himself. Before we walked in, we sat on stones near the garden, and he officially asked me to be his girlfriend. I thought I already was, but this was the first time I had ever been formally asked besides the random note with "check yes or no" in middle school. I, of course, said yes.

I could not believe this guy wanted to date me—a man with a job who looked like a model and had his life together. We celebrated with some kissing, but he wanted to go farther, and I stopped him. He called me a tease and said, "You can't do that to a guy unless you plan on going all the way." I felt guilty, so I gave in. I figured now that I was officially his girlfriend, he had the right to expect sex from me.

I figured now that I was officially his girlfriend, he had the right to expect sex from me.

It was not long before I was completely hooked on him. I didn't know if I was more addicted to sex or to him. Either way, my old habits of co-dependency soon kicked in. I couldn't see it, but he could. All my choices were now based on him: what he liked, where he was. I quit making my own decisions. Just a few weeks after we became official, I got my nails done for the first time, and I had them painted forest green. He looked at them in disgust and asked, "Why would you paint them that color?"

"It's your favorite color," I said. He hesitated. We moved on from the conversation but started arguing more frequently. Our most common disagreement was over my make-out sessions with Briana. He insisted that even though she was a girl, making out was still cheating. I refused to stop because the attention I was getting seemed more important than our relationship. But apparently, attention was important to him too.

He started talking to the girl who served nachos at the pool hall . . . a lot. She was older and exotic, and she was definitely more mature than I was in all areas. I started to become extremely jealous and clingy while his life was coming together nicely. He bought a house and a new Nissan 320z sports car, and I was becoming less important to him as he was getting all he wanted from life.

One night, he wrecked the car, and after the wreckage, he took a long hard look at what was wrong with his life. The biggest thing was me. Then came those dreaded words: "We need to talk." He said I had lost the personality that he was originally attracted to; I became too much like him and less like me. *It has to be the nacho girl*, I thought. But when I asked, he denied having any feelings for her.

I pretended not to care and went to Speedway to get attention. Speedway was a street where we all met to proudly race souped-up cars. Girls danced in the back of trucks or stood in front of the parked cars, flashing their breasts to the racers. I hopped in some random guy's Camaro to speed down the street, my stomach on a roller-coaster ride. I looked to my right to see if I saw anyone else worth hanging out with that night, but instead, out of the corner of my eye, I glimpsed a pair of very familiar figures making out. There he was: Pete with the "nacho" girl. We had just broken up! I was devastated.

I indulged my pain as I spent the next year getting trashed with his circle of friends. He was busy with *her*, so why shouldn't I get busy with his best friends? I had secretly hoped one of them would maybe fall in love with me, but none of them respected me. Why would they? All the while, I was still hooking up with Pete when he stopped by for one reason and one reason only. Until Bobby, that is.

DO YOU LOVE ME?

Bobby was a beautiful Latino man with green eyes who thought that I was "so much fun." We started dating around my birthday in September. Within weeks, we were alternating whose house we stayed at each night. We weren't having sex yet, but we were spending all our time together.

One night, we were fooling around. Like *déjà vu*, he wanted to go farther, but I wasn't ready for that. Angry, he explained what happens to a man who gets aroused and then has to stop. In pain and frustration, he, too, called me a tease. After a few minutes of pouting, I thought, *Why can't I get to know someone*

49

before they immediately demand sex? Still, I did not want him mad at me, so I gave in. The truth is, I *was* a tease. Even though I really wanted to wait for sex, I had a hard time doing so. I had always heard that the longer you made a guy wait, the longer he would stay around. So I would push every physical limit, trying to be careful not to go all the way, because I didn't want to be perceived as a slut.

We started going to parties with lots of cocaine, and I was invited to all the parties with his other friends. But when it was time to go back to Speedway for his ritual with the guys, I was not allowed out with him. He was friends with Pete and everyone else I had fooled around with in my efforts to get over him. He didn't want those guys to know our true dating status since I had made my way around the crew.

How I hated secret relationships! I desired someone who would be so thrilled to be with me that he would shout it from the rooftops. As with Pete's other friends, I seemed to be everyone's secret side girl. With the exception of Briana, of course, and other girlfriends I picked up each week at the pool hall. They had no problem using me to gain attention for themselves.

A few nights later, I discovered it wasn't about who *I* dated; it was about who *he* dated. His ex-girlfriend was possibly pregnant with his baby. On our evening out, he asked for a ride to her house. I didn't want to lose him because every other girl wanted this man I had somehow won over. So I waited in the car, sick to my stomach at the idea that he was possibly cheating on me. Then I gave him a ride home. Despite my anger, I didn't feel as if I deserved any better. He had happily trotted back to the car high and showed me how much extra weed he had. Ugh. I didn't want drugs. I wanted him and what I thought could be love! I still took his weed and tried to enjoy was left of our night together.

After two months of dating, he began to take me seriously. We went for drives and listened to Mark Anthony and Enrique Iglesias. We took late night swims at his apartment. I was falling madly for him. His birthday was coming up, and I wanted to get him a chain he loved. I didn't have any money, so without thinking twice, I went to the strip club where my sister worked and was immediately put on stage—no questions asked or paperwork needed. After one on-stage dance and one private lap dance, I made enough to buy the gift and booked out of the club before they could ask for my ID since I was only seventeen. He loved the gift, and I avoided answering how I paid for it.

A few nights later, we were at his best friend Virginia's house, wired on cocaine as usual. Bobby asked, "Do you love me?"

My jaw dropped in shock. "What? What would give you that idea?"

Everything in me recoiled at that four-letter word. I sat in my whirling discomfort as I absentmindedly processed my own verbal sidestep. I wasn't sure if the discomfort was directed more at myself or at all that love had never proven to be for me. At the very least, I hated the *word*. But I couldn't admit that I *was* falling in love with him. If I did, he might leave just like everyone else I thought I loved had done.

I brushed off his question. He spent the rest of the night in Virginia's room while I waited and hoped he'd come back to me. He eventually did, and I stopped worrying for the moment.

A TRAGIC ACCIDENT

As the relationship kept progressing, I began to take school more seriously. I was testing out of classes and flying through high school. I got into honors math and language classes, and my teacher nominated me for the Women's National Math and Science Initiative. I was also accepted as a participant in an internship for young entrepreneurs.

Attending an alternative school allowed me to move at my own pace. I could go as fast as I needed, which helped me stay focused due to my ADHD. Any time I slowed down, I became distracted and was soon suspended for missing school because of partying. Here, I could go twice as fast to make up for lost time. I loved school, and if I could go through the classes quickly enough, my mind would stay occupied so that I didn't get in trouble.

I met with my intern group, and we decided to start a magazine. I loved to write, organize, and market, so this internship was a great fit for me. As I was about to finish for the day, I got a message from Bobby, asking me to pick him up. *Wow*, I thought. *He is with the guys, and he is going to let me pick him up! We must be getting serious.* He had left behind his favorite baseball hat a few days earlier, so I grabbed it and picked up a pizza.

I drove for about an hour out to where they were all riding ATVs. I was *so* excited, I missed the turn. I had to drive for another mile before I could turn around. But when I finally found a place to turn back to the road, I kept running into detours. I was supposed to meet him at a store called Sam Rose. But when I arrived, the scene was laden with caution tape and cops. *What's going on?* I tried to drive down each neighborhood street, but they were all blocked off because of whatever had happened. I was late, and I hated being late!

Finally, frustrated at the delays and with a foreboding curiosity about the blockaded entrance, I parked my car a few streets away from the store and started walking. People were gathered in the street in front of Sam Rose. Navigating through the crowd, I looked around distractedly until an unexpected sight caught my attention and halted me in my tracks. A few feet short of the stop sign near the store, an ATV was flipped upside down in the road. No one was anywhere near it. The sight began to register in mind, and a sudden chill raised the hair on my arms. *An ATV*, I thought. *A riderless, flipped ATV.* My pulse raced as my mind stumbled over the obvious facts in front of me. I started running toward the scene.

"Where is Bobby?" The words tumbled out, laced with tight, strangled alarm.

A sheet covered up someone in the middle of the road near the stop sign. Without thinking, in the same moment, I screamed and lurched forward. The police rushed to hold me back. "Is it Bobby?" My loud cry demanded an answer. Alarm turned to full-blown panic, and my words became rushed and hysterical shrieks. "Let me talk to him! Right now! I need answers! Why isn't anyone telling me what is going on?" My stomach churned, and my vision swam while I blocked the truth from settling into my heart.

I had to do something, anything, no matter how irrational. I called his friends one after another and left hysterical voicemails, crying and explaining that something had happened to Bobby . . . but I wasn't sure what. While I was frantically trying to describe the scene to someone over voicemail, the police finally pulled me aside. I forgot to close the phone and disconnect the call, and the voicemail tape rolled on, capturing the exchange that followed.

"I'm sorry, miss," said a cop. He glanced around the scene and refusing to meet my eyes. He kicked at a loose stone on the road with the toe of his boot. In my desperation for information, his approach took even longer. Finally, he refocused his gaze on me and continued. "The gentleman who was riding that four-wheeler lost control. It appears he flew off, and he wasn't wearing a helmet. Another car may have been involved, but they left the scene. We are currently looking for witnesses." I blinked, pushing through the fog in my brain to grasp his words. *Breathe, Deanna. You can do this. Find out as much information as possible. Figure out what step is next. Then take action. Now we're getting somewhere.*

I hadn't yet realized what the sheet covering him meant. "Did he make it? Can I see him?" My hopeful words were like an eerie echo of a younger girl whose world had not yet been shattered by loss. A younger girl with glasses to show a mother whose eyes would never open again. How quickly my hope turned to cold, empty horror at the officer's direct reply.

"No. He is dead."

I screamed and dropped to my knees as all the air left my chest. My stomach felt as if I had been punched in the gut, and the pain radiated in waves. Overcome with the debilitating darkness of the truth, I couldn't even stand. I sobbed while the voicemail recording captured my despair. I hung up the phone and finally managed to climb to my feet. I weakly stumbled toward the crash scene, collapsing when I reached it. Grief counselors were already there, quickly invading my space and attempting to talk to me.

"Get out of my face!" I yelled with blind contempt for their kindness. "Let me go be with him, *pleeassse!*" I choked out the desperate words, pleading for a mercy that would not be granted.

I don't know how long I sat there, numb to the people and movement around me, drowning in my pain. My sister eventually arrived with her boyfriend. The authorities must've called her since my dad was out of town for work. She was my only nearby family. Still in a daze, I walked with her to the car, dragging my feet weighed down with sorrow. We went with the police to Bobby's mom's house to break the news.

・・・・・・・・・・ ◇ ・・・・・・・・・・・

I don't know how long I sat there, numb to the people and movement around me, drowning in my pain.

・・・・・・・・・・ ◇ ・・・・・・・・・・・

The funeral was a few days later. Just like at my mom's funeral, I decided to sing Bobby one last song. Singing and writing were the only ways I knew how to connect to my emotions. I picked a song by Sara Evans, "There's No Place That Far." Once again, it was an open-casket viewing. I was mortified. They had to reconstruct his face due to the damage he suffered from flipping off the four-wheeler, hitting the road, and possibly being run over. I closed my eyes and dropped my senior picture in his casket.

In the following months, I was a complete wreck, lost all focus, and stopped going to school. My friend from the internship program quit attending as well. Since he was homeless and living in a storage facility, he had all the free time in the world to spend with me while I grieved. We drove around aimlessly, listening to Pearl Jam "Where, Oh Where Could My Baby Be?" on repeat.

I missed so much school that I was almost suspended. The girls waited in the parking lot but not to offer the comfort I needed. "You know Bobby didn't love you, right? He was still seeing his ex. You know, the one about to have his baby. You better watch your back because she just got transferred here."

Could this get any worse? Will I ever feel safe? Respected? Loved? In my even more distraught state, I nodded and headed to my class.

"We're just trying to help."

Sure you are. Their comments felt anything but helpful, as if they were cutting me off at the knees when I was already down. I walked away from their snickers, pulled out my books, and spent most of my days crying tears of senseless pain at my desk. My Discman was blaring Puff Daddy's, "I'll Be Missing You," a good-bye song written to The Notorious B.I.G.

After school, I went to his grave and had a beer with him by pouring his out on the ground. I lit cigarettes for both of us, put his in the ground until it burned out, and proceeded to tell him about my day. Some days, I would sleep there. A family friend helped me record his last voicemail and put it on cassette. I could now listen to his voice whenever I wanted.

I couldn't let go. I could no longer show myself at the pool hall or at any other place we frequented. I retreated into myself and put my nose to the books, ignoring everyone and everything around me. I had one goal: to finish this season of my life despite the pain.

CHAPTER SIX

LAUNCHING MY CAREER

THE CUT OFF for those of us who wanted to walk in the spring commencement was approaching. I managed to stay focused long enough to be eligible for early graduation at the end of my junior year. Almost all my assignments were completed, so I wasn't spending much time at school. I was ready to get serious about life while I finished what would be my final year. My goal was to work toward full independence and pursue my dreams. I wanted to take care of myself and have control of my life. Since I didn't have many classes, I picked up a few jobs. Productivity could typically keep me out of trouble.

At night, I worked at a call center until early in the morning, doing surveys with people from all over the world, but mainly Australia. "On a scale of 1–10, how would you rate your current satisfaction with your insurance company?" Each time someone finished the entire survey, I got a bonus. I loved hitting company-based goals. This job afforded me confidence, as well as free days and weekends off to go after even more for myself.

So I pursued acting and modeling through a local talent agency, which was a dream I had shared with Bobby before he died. He had wanted me to follow my dreams, but I was too enamored with him to think of much else. Now I had all the time in the world to focus on me. I learned how to audition and started working on skills to fill my talent resume. Unfortunately, the amount of acting classes I could afford didn't take up much of my time. While waiting for that dream to unfold, I looked for another job to keep myself busy—a job where I could be discovered.

I walked in the restaurant, and I knew my search was over. The misters under the bright orange awning were spraying the wooden deck while I handed in my application. All eyes were on me. The men looked at me like fresh meat to lust over, and the girls stared with contempt. Chicken wings were frying, football was on the TVs, and the sex appeal of the entire operation was enough to fill my need for validation. I had picked what I thought was the next best thing to becoming a model. *This is great*, I thought. *This restaurant only picks the best-looking girls.* Getting hired was the ultimate validation. The very body parts I spent most of my childhood ashamed of not having were now my greatest assets, *and* I got to show them off in a skintight, low-cut tank top. With the right push-up bra, I looked as if I had a boob job at seventeen.

> *My addiction was strong enough that I was willing to risk my life over it. I used drugs to get men and used men to get drugs.*

Once hired, I attended all the after-work parties and continued in my promiscuous ways, which the men liked. But some of the waitresses hated me for this behavior. I didn't understand it. They were all doing the same thing, so what was their problem with me? Was it because I was still in high school, and the whole restaurant could get in trouble? They told me that I was fake. They said I only pretended to be a good, smart girl, and I was nothing more than a tramp. Apparently to sleep around, you had to have a nasty personality, too, which I didn't. I still loved people. But I had self-worth issues. More than that, I was an addict—addicted to people, attention, and approval.

My addiction was strong enough that I was willing to risk my life over it. I used drugs to get men and used men to get drugs. I became more involved with one of the cooks named Max. I showed up for countless after-work parties at his place that involved beer bongs and other bongs. He encouraged me to put on a show for him and his friends to prove how much I liked him. But after I gave in to his requests, they lost respect for me anyhow. I then had to fight even harder to win his attention. That was the beginning of an extremely sick cycle.

We fueled each other's co-dependency and masked this enabling behavior under the pretense of supposedly understanding each other. We bragged about who was on more medications for various mental illnesses. If I was going through a phase of cutting my wrists, he would cut his more deeply. If we were going on a drive, he would turn Godsmack all the way up and slam on the gas, playing chicken with our lives to see who would crack first. I wasn't sure I would make it to my graduation alive, but at this point in life, I didn't know of any other way to live.

One night, I was barely hanging on mentally when we went on a walk, just the two of us. I was expressing how the relationship was making me feel about myself. He stopped the conversation, pulled out a 9mm gun and pointed it at himself and then at me. "If you really feel like dying," he said, "then go ahead and pull the trigger now." I cried hysterically, hoping he would comfort me as I stood there, trembling. I had opened up and been honest about my feelings, and instead of reciprocating by sharing his thoughts, he suggested that I end my life then and there. Then he twisted the conversation and made it about him, threatening to kill himself as well. This was a regular occurrence, but I continued to stay with him because I felt as if he accepted me, dysfunction and all. He was also a single dad who deeply loved his little girl. I figured these positive qualities outweighed any of his flaws. I couldn't see past my own dysfunction to recognize his unhealthy behavior.

The relationship eventually went south, but I continued showing up to work as if it were no big deal. Maybe if I could become one of the most popular girls, he would realize what he had lost. This restaurant portrayed itself as a classy joint that could help launch a public career in modeling if we played our cards right. They had rules that ranged from how we wore our hair to regulating our public behavior. Although our uniforms left practically nothing to the imagination, if we were caught dancing at a strip club after hours, we would be fired. Some of us had high goals of making it into nude magazines like the girls we saw in the picture frames hung around the restaurant. So at least on the surface, we had to stay classy.

One sunny day, the right opportunity presented itself. My manager encouraged me to enter a swimsuit competition to represent our store. The winner of this competition would win a nude layout in a well-known porn magazine. Since I was still seventeen, I knew the layout wouldn't be an option. Even so, I saw this as the next step to being discovered. Here was a chance for me to practice modeling and walking down a runway since the talent agency I had been working with was taking my money without giving me real work in return.

My dad was my biggest fan. He eagerly showed up at the competition to support me. At the time, I had no idea that most fathers would discourage this type of work. To me, it seemed no different than when he showed up at my other events: baton twirling in parades, cheerleading during football games, and now, this swimsuit competition that could lead to a career in porn. Sometimes he traveled for work, so he couldn't always attend my events. When he did attend, it meant even more to me. Neither of us found the swimsuit competition leading to a porn career awkward.

Our home still had few boundaries when it came to expressing sexuality. Dad was an attractive, single man, and we often found him sleeping with our friends' parents and any other women close to our family. We had known some of them for years and years, so we struggled as we watched him sabotage these relationships. By the time we were teenagers, he was going to the same strip club where my sister worked (though not to see her) and bar hopping with my surgically enhanced co-workers. As a family, we seemed to have an understanding with one another about these matters. We didn't say anything about his behaviors, and he didn't say anything about our vocational endeavors. So there he sat, cheering me on as I continued to work for the attention I craved.

THE GATEWAY

While waitressing at this establishment, I learned about acceptable ways to sell sex, in addition to posing for nude magazines. Part of this involved prostitution, only the other waitresses disguised this as finding sugar daddies. Two of my coworkers, each with two kids to feed, did whatever it took to earn money. They had an acquired lifestyle that encouraged them to enlist the financial support of rich men.

One night, we went to the bars, and they willingly snuck me in. After they hung out with my dad, we came back to their house. A man was waiting in Kristen's bed. "I'm in a lot of pain from cramps," she said. "Would you mind taking care of him? He's going to pay me a lot of money. I really need it this month for my kids." My codependency kicked into high gear. I took care of business for her and officially turned my first trick.

Prostituting was a dizzying mix of demoralizing and empowering. *I am now getting paid for doing what I already end up doing when I'm drunk*, I thought. I stayed with Kristen for many more nights to take advantage of the new lifestyle of earning money and drinking whatever I wanted, whenever I wanted. Pretending to be an adult was fun. Hanging out with girls that commanded the attention of every man in the room—and got it—was exhilarating. I wanted to be exactly like them, and I sure did try.

◇

My first X-rated movie was created for someone's personal stash.

◇

While playing a game of Power Hour (drinking a shot of beer per minute), we ran out of beer. But the neighbors were having a party, so I headed upstairs to introduce myself, when we found we already knew each other from my first high school. These same boys who used to make fun of me were now men. I was in luck; a big bottle of Everclear awaited me on the kitchen counter. After a few shots, I was ready to entertain the whole house and prove I was no longer that underdeveloped shrimpy girl from freshman year. It all happened so quickly, and I figured no one would know . . . except the other neighbor showed up at the party and recorded the entire thing on video. My first X-rated movie was created for someone's personal stash. *Well, everyone at high school was right*, I thought the next day, when I put together the pieces of the night before. *I am a slut, just like they said.*

Drinking was no longer enough to satisfy the sickness inside me. My friends were not into hard drugs, but even so, I found my way back to them. Kristen's brother was addicted to crack. We got along great—so much so that he introduced me to his drug of choice. Within seconds, I was instantly hooked and ready to sell myself and everything I owned to keep my high going.

Using all the tools I had at my disposal, I went next door to find the guy who had filmed my drunken charade. I offered my new services in exchange for some money. *I mean, doesn't everyone do this?* He said he would not pay me; he only wanted to have sex with me if I actually wanted to. I needed to stay high, so I sold him some of my things instead. I was willing to do anything to forget about how my life was turning out.

UPSIDE DOWN

I was physically and emotionally crashing from drugs and unfulfilled dreams as I went back to delivering wings. I had resolved to only partake in what I thought was normal after-work drinking. I played it cool for a few nights to prove I could handle hanging out with of-age drinkers. Then I was invited to a party way outside the city. I called up an ex-girlfriend from a very brief fling to be my designated driver and partner in entertainment. But she ended up drinking even more than I did—Zimas. After we made drunk fools of ourselves at the party, we were ready to drive home, which was an hour away. No one at the party was sober enough to stop us. It was rainy, and the roads were slick and curvy as we sped along at about sixty miles per hour.

"What are you doing?" I demanded loudly as the car veered off the road.

"I saw a deeerrrr!" She screamed, before her voice was completely muffled under an unnatural symphony of destruction.

My car flipped three times before we finally landed upside down, far from the road and trapped in the vehicle. I started banging on the windows and kicking the windshield, trying to get out of my now-totaled 1988 Maroon Chevy Cavalier. *I love this car. My dad worked hard to restore it so that it looked just like my mom's maroon Stanza. Now it's totaled,* I thought. Lucid thoughts of disappointment blocked out the emotional shock and physical tremors still lingering from the impact. But then a sinister crack filled the air and tugged my attention back to my immediate surroundings. "What was that noise?" I cried in distress. "Is this car going to explode?" Sensing danger despite our disorientation, our alarm drove us to action.

Somehow, although we were upside-down and in an alcohol-impaired panic, we escaped the vehicle and staggered to the side of the road. By some miracle, a stranger saw us, pulled over, and called an ambulance. As I waited for emergency assistance to arrive, I took a few steps away from everyone, bent down, and forced myself to throw up as much alcohol as possible, hoping to minimize any alcohol poisoning. My head grew dizzy, and my throat burned, and I started to black out. I remember lying in the ambulance, but I have no recollection of anything after that—until I woke up in the hospital with my dad seated next to my bed. The whirring of machines and constant beeps of the medical environment were not new to me. An exhausted, bone-deep shame greeted me as I had awakened this way before. By the time the paramedics tested our blood-alcohol-content level, my friend's was off the charts, but mine had dropped. *Should I congratulate myself for this questionable achievement?*

My dad whispered to me, "Your friend has a drinking problem." Numbness wrapped itself around my soul. I agreed all too easily and played the victim.

It somehow seemed fitting that we lost the car modeled after mom's in a drunken crash that night. Dad had wrecked hers in much the same manner. It was one more sign that no matter how hard I tried, my life was going nowhere but deeper down a repeating loop of failures, addictions, and shame.

7

OVER THE LINE

FINALLY! The excitement of our pending graduation filled the air—and this, of course, justified celebrating all weekend. So I showed up to my graduation out of my mind on cocaine. My sister, twenty-one, and I, seventeen, were fighting as usual. I don't know if she was madder that I was high on such a significant day or that I was graduating with her. She'd asked me not to graduate early, because she wanted to be the first one of us to graduate. Honestly, I couldn't have been more proud of her for going back and finishing school, all while raising a baby and facing other challenges. But I had my own goals to accomplish. So I graduated with her and dealt with her resulting anger. My love and encouragement were not enough for her; everything had to be a competition.

She moved to Indiana that summer after graduation. I, on the other hand, turned eighteen and officially moved in with Kristen. I decided to quit all my extra jobs so I could pick up more shifts at the restaurant. With my new-found freedom, I could afford to attend a party at an old neighbor's house. She was one of the few girls my age I had respected growing up. I felt safe with her and escaped to her house when the drama in own home was too much. She knew how to have healthy fun and was always kind and welcoming to me.

She introduced me to a nice military boy named Josh. We hit it off and started drinking together and then dating. In addition to his great personality, he also got along well with my dad and honestly seemed to like me. I didn't know what to do with such a relatively healthy relationship. I actually liked him so much that I did not want to have sex with him, because I felt it would ruin our relationship. I wanted something real—terrified as I was of it. Unfortunately, despite my deepest desires, I withheld myself from Josh due to my fear of intimacy. But I still looked other places for relationships.

Though I had my own dark secrets, for a while, we maintained what seemed to be a normal, happy relationship. Soon after Josh and I started dating, I introduced my new coworker Heather to Josh's friend, Ken. The four of us spent a lot of quality time together. One day, we discovered that even though we had grown up in different states, none of us had ever been to the beach. Since we were good friends delighted by the idea of adventure, we took a road trip to experience the beach for the first time. We all shared a hotel room, and I was still so afraid of sleeping with my boyfriend that I slept under the sink instead of in the bed with him.

In the morning, we finally reached the beach, and I fell completely in love with the ocean—the scent, the look, the sound, and the freedom—it was all more than I had ever imagined. I called my godmother, a woman who invited us into her family after Mom died. I told her I wasn't coming home. I knew she would understand that I wanted to start a fresh life since she had, after all, watched me go through one horror after another growing up. After I hung up, I walked into a restaurant on the beach and applied to work there since it was part of the same chain. Then I called the Arizona location to let them know I would not be coming back to work the next week. I broke up with Josh and sent him and our friends all on their way. I found a man on the beach who seemed nice enough and asked to move in with him. But within twenty-four hours, the novelty of the staying in California wore off, and I came back to the hotel with my tail between my legs, asking if I could have a ride home. Except I now had no job to crawl back to.

On the drive home, I swallowed what little pride I had left, but I still couldn't help feeling as if I were meant to stay in Los Angeles. Even so, I was resigned to returning to Arizona. *Oh well, back to parties and affairs.* I called my ex-boyfriend Max and stayed with him for a few days. Finally, I let Josh off the hook and lied to him so that he could move on. I told him I might be pregnant, and since we had not had sex, he knew it wasn't his. I wasn't really pregnant, but this announcement was merely another part of my sick game to try to win Max back. *He* was the one who understood I was sick and loved me anyway.

NEW BEGINNINGS

I decided to try and go to college since I had just graduated from high school. I tested back into honors classes and was excited to be on my way to finishing college early, just like I'd finished high school early. It was time for another fresh start and new experiences, so I signed up for activities, boards, and committees—anything to stay involved and dedicated to this new phase.

A few weeks after starting school, I drove to Max's, thrilled with the new experiences I was having. We planned to go on an adventure to celebrate with his four roommates. We took one of his classic Ford trucks and loaded it up with all the guns we had in the apartment to go shooting. As we rolled around the corner of the mountain, a car was coming straight for us as if in slow motion. He hit us head on, and yet we somehow barely missed going off the mountain. The other driver was terrified at the sight of a truck filled with guns. But we stepped away from the guns, took his insurance information, and let him go on his way. I knew a lawyer's son who had frequented our restaurant, so this was an easy lawsuit for all of us.

The trauma of the head-on collision gave me the excuse I needed to give up on all my new dreams and start taking drugs again, supposedly for pain. I dropped out of college, quit the cheer squad I had helped start, and got a second job at a windshield company that had hired me as purely office eye-candy. The owner paid me to date him, sit on his lap at work, and be around him. But I never slept with him. He was married and seemed to draw the line there. No matter—I was thrilled to have an administrative job. I loved to work and be useful. And if I got in the door by being eye-candy, so be it. Eventually, I partied too much and just stopped showing up to work all together. If my dreams interfered with my party lifestyle, they were not dreams worth having.

A few weeks later, while reading the local paper, I came across an ad that said "models wanted, accepting applications at the tanning salon." I told Kristen, and together, we decided to check it out. But this was different from your average tanning facility. It was also a costume and prop shop for strippers. All sex industry workers got 10 percent off everything in the store, including tanning, to help keep up their image for business.

Employees also got to model the lingerie and swimwear at another local restaurant chain. The best part about the gig was that the bartenders assumed that since I was a lingerie model, I must be old enough to drink. So I'd partake in a few shots at the bar before changing and modeling for the people as they ate and drank. *This could finally be my big break into modeling!* I thought. And it turned out, I was right. Well, kind of.

CROSSING THE LINE

My big break just so happened to be waiting at a table in the bar lounge. From his seat, Brody's dark and calculating eyes roved over me, on a search for a new woman to bring into his circle of wealth. His power allowed him to sit and look, to wait while another fetched his prey. In fact, a beautiful, classy-looking Asian woman introduced me to him once his eyes had drunk their fill and his appraisal was complete. Indifferent, he acted as if as if my answer mattered little. He then told me that I could make more money modeling with him than I could working at the tanning salon. Somehow, the cool confidence in his words was as seductive as it was sinister. The slight acceleration of my pulse confirmed within me what his demeanor conveyed: Brody could accomplish whatever he said he could. Some strange force and the swirling waters of whispered promises pulled me toward him. I agreed to give it a try.

He started me out with some motorcycle and car ads, and he was right. I was making more money, *and* I was finally an actual model with a print ad. Pride swelled within my chest as I looked at my own figure reflected on the page. Such success was a new kind of drug—one that lowered inhibitions and boundaries—and any remaining personal standards. Success quieted any misgivings as I earned more money and as Brody steered me toward gigs that involved less and less clothing. He brought bottles of expensive liquor to each job, anything I wanted. Before long, I was making amateur porn while more hungry eyes than ever fixed themselves shamelessly on me. I turned a blind eye to the spiraling downward momentum.

Around that time, I had been dating a man named Tim who also used to be a frequent customer at the restaurant I previously worked at. But our time together—which, of course, was dramatic and emotional and marked by our co-dependency with one another—left me lonely and frustrated. So one night, I called my ex-boyfriend, Max, to meet him at his house for some drinks. A couple of hours into our chill, uncomplicated night, two people walked in who would change my life for the worse, as if that were even possible.

Success quieted any misgivings as I earned more money and as Brody steered me toward gigs that involved less and less clothing.

Tia and Rob were what we called tweekers (meth addicts), and they had stopped by to sell us some weed. My eyes lit up at the other drugs they had. I wanted desperately to get out of myself for the weekend. Max saw the look in my eyes and warned me, "Deanna, if you leave with those two, I know I'm going to lose you forever. I've been down that road. It's dangerous. I don't want to see you fight that battle."

What's the big deal, I thought? *I've done every kind of drug at this point. What new drugs could they possibly have to offer me?* And in fact, it wasn't the drug that was different; it was how I *did* the drug that was different. I didn't have to destroy my nose and give up being able to breathe to get the high I was looking for. Instead of a straw, they handed me a pipe and took me to the house of someone who taught me how to use it. They supplied me with enough meth to get me officially hooked, all *for free.* I stayed awake all weekend. Once my free ride ended, I had to find a way to come up with some cash. I ended up selling Max's prized ring, my phone, and whatever else I could find to get more drugs.

69

I was horribly depressed when I came down a few days later. I had disappeared with no explanation, and when I had to face both my boyfriend and my ex-boyfriend, I lied and said I got high by being in a room with other people who were smoking it. Neither of them believed me and quit talking to me. I figured that would be the last time I would touch that drug, but only a week later, I came back with more possessions to sell and bought more meth. That summer, I could not stay away from meth for more than a week or so. Week after week, I repeated the pattern. Quit. Start. Quit. Start. I told people each time that this was my last time, not wanting them to know that I was already addicted, and I only had so much money. The dealers were discounting drugs to keep me coming back.

After months of the back and forth, the drug dealers became enraged with me. I did not want to mess with these people who were rumored to hog-tie people and drop them off in the desert. So I had to start paying full price. Brody, now my agent, pimped me out at all hours of the night since I needed the money. There was no more hiding our motives behind acting or modeling. He set me up in a hotel room, and every half an hour, a new person came knocking on the door as he waited outside with his gun ready.

He set me up in a hotel room, and every half an hour, a new person came knocking on the door as he waited outside with his gun ready.

If I wasn't making money, I was dating the person with the drugs. So I began to date Ben, a friend of Tia and Rob's. Our drug use was progressive as were our fraudulent behaviors. In this circle, no one had real names or IDs, so they stole one identity after another by taking mail from people. They washed any handwritten checks with chemicals and rewrote the amounts. Then they gave the doctored checks to me to cash since I was a female and I looked so innocent. They also used me as bait to distract guys at the counters of convenience stores while I waited for them to make change for a freshly made, counterfeit one-hundred-dollar bill.

LIFE ON THE STREET

I was now officially in the street game. Each week, Ben and I were squatting basketball courts, unoccupied houses, and hotels—and doing whatever else we needed to find a place to sit while I stayed up doing drugs for days on end. When the drugs ran out, my pimp was ready with new clients. Since the demand for me was increasing, he set me up with higher-paying clients.

Some nights, I was in so much physical pain from how these men treated me that I could only lay there, crying and bleeding, as multiple people from all types of backgrounds and vocations came to take advantage of me. On one such night, a client complained to my pimp that he didn't get what he came for. My body had shut down completely as did I. But I knew my job well, and I knew I could provide the only thing that was ever wanted from me anyway. It wasn't as if I were being asked to make some sort of emotional connection with these men, which would have been impossible for me. So I pulled it together to do my job, but because of my drama, this client didn't pay my pimp. This unleashed uncommon anger from my pimp—who was normally quite controlled—and the night took an ugly turn.

Ben was waiting outside in the car. I had told him I was a massage therapist, and he pretended to believe that and happily waited for me at work, then spent my money on more drugs. He came in to use the bathroom before taking off to meet our dealer. When he left, Brody realized his phone was gone, and suddenly my life was on the line. He looked at me, and I thought I was standing in front of the devil himself. In his deepest, angriest, most terrifying voice, he told me, "If you don't find that phone, you and all your druggie friends are dead!" I knew he meant every word. I called Ben, crying, but he had already sold the phone to a person who had immediately sold it again. Each person knew the threats of my pimp were for real, and if that phone was not returned, we'd all be severely hurt or dead. Luckily, the phone was tracked down. I escaped a pimp's wrath, but he was done with me and my drama, so he cut me loose to the street.

Surprisingly, that was the least of the insanity I was living in. Outside of prostitution, my social life took extreme turns. One day, my friends and I were smoking meth with a new friend, only to find out the next day that he had been

71

shot and killed. Then the next week, we were doing drugs with the people that shot him. All of us were too afraid to bring it up in fear we would be next. In this world, people were put into trunks and disappeared. While I was treading these dangerously thin lines, I was joyriding and hiding out in people's vans and U-Hauls with no idea how I had been trapped into this face-picking, shadow-chasing, psychotic world.

One Thursday afternoon, I took a break from my usual habit of sitting in a stranger's bathroom sink, completely fixated on picking my face for hours on end. I headed to a nearby pool hall to reminisce. While there, I ran into a former high school peer, who greeted me with unconcealed shock. "Deanna," she breathed out in disbelief. "You used to be so pretty." An almost imperceptible pause came before a penetrating question pierced my heart. "What did you do?"

I turned my full profile toward her as the question hung suspended between us. I looked directly at her so she could see the sores covering my face, some still bleeding, some scabbed over. My heart hid just behind my own hollow gaze. She assessed me, taking in every bit of my seventy-eight-pound, worn-down frame. She *really* saw me—saw me in a way few people did anymore, now that I lived in the world where everyone looked without seeing. As if outside myself, my large, empty eyes slowly blinked while my battered mind processed the scene. Struck by the honesty of the moment, the deep, numbed, forgotten recesses of my soul slipped out of hiding. I admitted the truth for the first time out loud. The truth that was buried but that I knew deep within: "This is what I've always felt like on the inside."

As I spoke, I felt sick and no longer wanted to exist. When those familiar feelings enveloped me, I knew it was time to pay a visit to the family psychiatrist I had seen for years. He had worked with my mom too. I went in for an appointment a few days later, and he told me my response to this girl was "rather interesting." He recognized the patterns: the incessant picking, random piercings, and the on-going self-mutilating I had started at fourteen. He had seen my mom go through similar cycles. After further discussion, he put me on more antipsychotics and antidepressants. But the drugs didn't help. Still out of my mind and with no real relief in sight, I turned my life back over to meth.

CHAPTER EIGHT

ARRESTED

A BAD OVERDOSE compounded by severe hallucinations landed me in the psych and detox ward. After seven days, I was pronounced cured and sent home. Cured was far from true, however, since I was drinking again a few hours later, still obsessed with using. After only a couple drinks, I was on the hunt to get my hands on my drug of choice. Only this time, I wanted more of it, and I wanted it faster. Other addicts warned me not to go down this path. Detached from what was happening, I was fascinated with how addicts judged other addicts for what drug they used or how they used it. Nearly everyone minimized and justified their own addictions by comparing themselves to others who seemed worse off. Even so, I didn't truly care. Instead, I surrendered to my new life as a junkie, the kind who willingly shared needles with diseased strangers if that's what it took for chemical escape that night. Since my future would likely end in death, the risks counted little.

When I ran out of drugs and supplies, a friend took me to the new dealer on the street. When we got to the apartment, it looked like any other apartment, but no one could have guessed what was going on inside. All of a sudden, out she came: my new fascination. Or was this a he? I didn't know what was going on. The person standing before me was forty years old, my dad's age. He was actually a man dressed as a woman who went by the name Missy. In no time at all, Missy became both my new dealer and my newfound obsession. I had been told my entire childhood that I would be gay, but I had spent my adult life insanely addicted to men. Now I finally had an answer to my confusion about my sexual preference. I decided, "This is great! Missy is the best of both worlds."

After our deal, Missy told me that he was off to go beat someone with some sort of tool, and I immediately thought, *Great! I won't need protection if I stay close to this one!*

And I was right. I wouldn't need protection—except, eventually, *from* him. As the relationship unfolded, so did his true abusive nature. By the time I encountered this side of him, though, I did not even have the option of running home to my father. Anytime I tried, Missy stopped me—literally and physically stopped me. He pushed me away from the door, kept the phone from me, and did whatever it took to keep me with him.

One night, my dad came searching for me because he hadn't heard from me in a month. He somehow found us at someone's evicted apartment where we were squatting in a drug trade. My dad was surprised when a large man in a pink nightgown opened the door, but he quickly handed Missy a stack of newspapers. "In case Deanna is looking for a job," he said, "I thought I would bring these over." Then he left.

A job? Who needed a job? I had a transvestite who went dumpster-diving at night, and when I was lucky, he found kids' clothes that were little enough for me to wear. He also came back with a whole bunch of stuff to sell on the street, mostly electronics. I did my part by spending all hours of the night organizing what he found. He furnished the apartment with this free stuff, and what he didn't find, he stole, including our makeup, perfume, and hygiene supplies. While he was out, I was home, cleaning the temporary place for hours with a Q-tip. One night, my compulsive cleaning was interrupted by a loud and forceful pounding at the door.

Bang! Bang! "Police!! Everybody down!"

My fragile composure shattered, and my breath hitched in my throat. This was every addict's worst nightmare. *Why? Why did this have to happen when Missy wasn't here?* I wondered in distress, as my eyes skittered about the room, landing

74

on everything and nothing all at once. *Why was I left alone to be questioned by police?* With sweaty palms and a composure I didn't feel, I answered the door. Somehow, once I let them in and stammered through the answers to their questions, I escaped with a warning and was simply tossed back onto the street.

Unfortunately, it wasn't the last time I found myself in such a jam. Scenarios like this repeated regularly when I was with Missy. Within a week, Missy and I were pulled over in his stolen Jeep that happened to have new plates picked up from Mexico. The cops weren't concerned that a forty-year-old man dressed up as a woman was driving around with an eighteen-year-old girl. I wasn't wearing a seatbelt because the Jeep didn't have one, and I also had no identification, so they found that reason enough to take me in. They handcuffed me and put me in the back seat of the police car. Sitting there, I looked down and realized I couldn't go to jail in my newfound dumpster

The cops weren't concerned that a forty-year-old man dressed up as a woman was driving around with an eighteen-year-old girl.

pants. I looked like a clown, and I knew I would get beat up for looking so foolish. So I pulled some gymnastics to ease my legs through my cuffed arms in the back seat of the cop car and took them off. I was down to skimpy boxers.

At the station, the cops took mug shots of me and put me in a holding room. They tried to get information from me about the person I was calling my fiancé. Yes, fiancé. He'd stolen a pink ring that I wore as a promise that, one day, we would get married. But only, I had stipulated, if I got to wear the wedding dress. "I don't know his name," I told the cops.

"What do you mean, 'you don't know his name?' You said you were engaged to him."

"Yes, but no one gives anyone their real names on the street." Well, except for me, because I had nothing to hide—including my dad's house, his property, credit cards, and my deceased mother's identity. As far as I was concerned, it was all fair game for the taking on the streets. These were the only things I had of value to keep my high going. That way, they wouldn't have to do home invasions while I watched. If they were going to steal, I assumed it should be from me.

After I spent the night detoxing in an all-white, perfectly square room, the cops decided to release me. Missy picked me up outside the jail and reluctantly gave me some of his drugs in pity for my ordeal. But lo and behold, we would soon find ourselves in trouble with the police again.

BAD DEAL

We had found a new friend, Amy, who let us crash with her and her three-year-old as long as we supplied her with drugs. Serious fights began to take place when Missy yelled at me and ordered me around, using degrading names. Though the place we were staying was new, these kinds of fights certainly were not. He had even called me these names and yelled other profanities at me during my most vulnerable moments with him.

\Screaming and chasing me with a bloody syringe, he threatened me once again. "I didn't use that, I swear!" I screamed back at him, knowing full well why a needle would cause such a response. There were new rules now.

Missy was now no longer Missy. Instead, he called himself Leo and wanted to be the man in the relationship. And to him, being the man meant taking back dominance over me and all my affairs. He told me that I could smoke drugs but could no longer use needles. I had to be in tip-top shape.

As I watched him stand in front of me seething, I knew I had done nothing wrong. Amy was the one who'd been using needles, not me. A couple of times, I tried to help her, because at eight months pregnant, her veins had all collapsed. I knew if I didn't help her, she would kill herself or the baby (who she later lost anyway). But she continued to try to do it on her own, leaving blood everywhere. Her blood—not mine—was all over the bathroom counters, but Leo wouldn't listen to me. He insisted on yelling at me and reminding me that he was in charge now, and *he* said when, where, and how I could use his drugs. I went to another room in the house and sat in terror and remorse, trying to make friends with Amy's little girl, as they devised a new scheme to find some drugs.

Amy often acted hot and cold with us, however. In fact, she was the reason for more than one of my run-ins with the police. As was her habit, anytime she came down from a high and needed all the junkies out of her house, Amy called some of her friends who were cops to kick us out.

The first time her cop friends came, I was by myself, and as usual, Missy (Leo) was nowhere to be found. The police found all the drug-related paraphernalia, and I was charged with my first misdemeanor. I was dropped off at my dad's in the back of a cop car. My dad and I were both too ashamed of me to talk about the incident, so we didn't. I fell asleep on the couch, and Missy dropped by to pick me up the next day while my dad was at work. We knew it was only a matter of time; we would have a place to stay when Amy was ready to get high again.

The next time we stayed with Amy, she did not call the cops, but they came and found us anyway. They happened to be in the area because of a reported bomb threat. Neighbors and police were surrounding the house. This was not long after 9/11 in 2001, and bomb scares were taken very seriously. We were all evacuated from Amy's house, along with the entire neighborhood. The police released what looked like little robots. The robots uncovered some recently obtained pipe bombs in the garage and detonated them. I was shocked. I had known Amy and Leo were up to something—they had recently made some trades I begged them not to—but I did not know that they had hidden bombs in the same house where Amy's three-year-old slept.

The police questioned us. In my defense, I said, "Don't you think if I found a bowling ball with a candle wick in it, that I would have called you guys?" Since they were pipe bombs, that statement made me look like an idiot. My ignorant response about what a bomb looked like distracted them and took their attention off me. Leo came out dressed as Missy and used the same excuse. *You SOB!* I thought. *You got us into this. Are you kidding me?*

We were running once again. It was time to find a new place to live. In an effort to earn some respect from Leo in the midst of this whirlwind, I took some of the stuff he had stolen from his last dealer to set up a drug trade of my own. I was stepping up my game. I was no longer only going to be doing drugs *from* everyone else; now I was officially participating in the drug dealing.

But that was not how Leo saw it. Furious, he accused me of stealing from him. As his anger erupted, I was once again in fear for my life. Terrified of what he would do to me, I started obsessively digging my nails into my arms, hoping I would no longer feel my own unending agony. Leo ordered us all to get in the van to leave the scene of my deal. He made it clear I was no longer a part of this transaction. We loaded up, and the Michael Jackson song, "Smooth Criminal," came on the radio. I started belting out the chorus. Leo glared at me in the rearview mirror as he knew full well I was singing those words to him. My boldness in that moment stemmed from the cold fact that I didn't care if I died at that point.

I was of no value to Leo any more. On the way to my dad's house, he turned every corner sharper and faster. He dumped me off there. For all he cared, my dad could have me back. I took a plastic credit card and broke in through the front door, waiting for dad to come home. While I was coming down hard, hounded by my own wild fears, he finally arrived and made his famous delicious tacos with giant fried tortilla shells. He asked no questions but was simply glad and comforted I was home and alive.

In the midst of enjoying my food, a sudden ringing in my ears became so loud, I was sure I had lost my hearing. Blind panic ripped through me. My eyes still registered my dad—he was only a short reach away. I tried to focus on his mouth moving, but I couldn't hear a word he said. Hysterical, I screamed for him to help me. In my distress and disillusionment, he fed me and allowed me to pass out. I detoxed at home for three days.

THIS IS MY LIFE ON DRUGS

I was clean, sober, and on the up and up after four or five days of being home with my dad. Then out of nowhere, a craving completely overwhelmed me. It was as if I were an actor in one of those commercials of "this is your life

78

on drugs," destroying everything in sight. Dad went to work but locked up all the phones first. He finally had me home and knew I couldn't leave without a phone. I was possessed by the thought that I needed to get to a hospital before I ended up back on drugs; I just knew I was going crazy. So I took a crowbar, a hammer, and whatever else I could find to break into the room where the phones were. But all my efforts weren't working.

A bunch of commotion came from the kitchen. My transvestite ex-fiancé was trying to break in through the living room window to check on me. He stuck his head through the cat door and continued yelling until I let him in. I didn't know what was going on. First, he threw me away, and then he broke into my house so we could finish a fight from days ago. He doped me up to pacify me and took me away from my dad's again. He wanted to be the only man I turned to.

He doped me up to pacify me and took me away from my dad's again. He wanted to be the only man I turned to

Leo's temptation with drugs worked, and I voluntarily chose to leave with him that same morning. My dad had no idea where to find me, but I was too busy trying to stay high to care. And so I developed a sickening cycle in my life: run with Leo; do more meth; meet worse people; get raped by a stranger; make Leo angry; be abused by Leo; run back to my dad in fear; leave the safety of my dad's; and return to Leo. The cycle unearthed deeper levels of horror. Time and time again.

But one day, I was back with Leo, and he maliciously ate in front of me while I was starving. To feed his own enjoyment, he denied me food. His twisted pleasure at my wretched state hit me like a splash of cold water to the face, and something in me snapped. As a fissure opened within me, anger hot as lava burst through the crack. I was done.

He tried to restrain me as I reached for the phone to call for help. I smacked him over the head with it and demanded he take me home, wielding an or-else threat that I would yell so loudly the cops would race over to our location. Driven by his own rage, he stormed to the car to comply.

He was driving like a crazy person, flying around corners in hopes that I'd tell him to calm down, apologize, and ask him to take me back to the motel. But I didn't. I held on, facing the danger, seething silently. We made it all the way to my dad's house. Leo fought to keep me from leaving the car. But my conviction had not lessened—I really *was* done this time. Done being pushed around. Done crawling back to him. He would have no more chances to break in when my dad was gone to get me high and get me out of there.

As the resolve built like a tidal wave in my chest, I knew one more thing with intense certainty. I was done running home to my dad's—done rushing into the bathroom of his house to end my life when I couldn't take it anymore. I could no longer listen to my dad bang on the door and cry in the hallway as I left the same bloody messes my mom made during her suicide attempts. I had been flying in and out of my dad's life whenever Leo threatened mine, and he was always there to clean up my mess. When I got out of the car, I didn't walk to the door.

Instead, I ran to my neighbor's for help, but she wouldn't let me in. She wasn't going to enable my behavior anymore. I assured her that I'd been off meth for two days. "Please, let me in. This guy is going to kill me! I just need to use your phone to get to safety. If I use the phone at my dad's, Leo will come back for me, but he won't make a scene at your house!"

She let me in, and determined to start on a new path, I called good old Max, the very person who had warned me to never get involved with this life. He pulled up with a friend to offer back up. They both were happy to help as they loved a challenge. They swung into the driveway in a 1980 Camaro, packed and ready to go, in case Leo came back for me. We peeled out of the driveway and drove forty minutes away. I moved back in with Max where I was safe. Where Leo couldn't break in and dope me up like he had done at my dad's. Here, somebody was watching me 24/7; I was too vulnerable to stay alone.

Once in a while, Max and his friends walked outside, packing loaded guns and carrying bats to make sure no one was looking for me. Max watched over me until I got better. He did not even let me get a job. He said I needed to get clean and focus on that. I got back on all my meds and ate until I reached a healthy weight. I began to almost feel human again. One day, he looked me in the eyes and said, "I told you. I told you if you left with those two, you wouldn't come back. Why didn't you listen?" He continued to say this every day as he nursed me back to health. I didn't mind, though, because I finally had the attention and care I had wanted from him—or any man—all along.

CHAPTER NINE

OUT OF OPTIONS

I HAD BEEN SOBER for four weeks when I decided to address my accumulated legal affairs. I took my number at the court and sat in my seat to wait, squirming with anxiety. I came to pay my fines and get my driver's license back so that I could leave. My dad wouldn't pay them for me this time. He insisted that I learn my lesson.

Though I didn't consciously know why, panic in my gut hinted at danger. I sat there like a doe caught in crosshairs, unaware warrants were out for my arrest. Random words floated through the air: fines, arrest, jail, and deadlines. I didn't know what all that meant, but my imagination didn't need the details to partner with my panic.

The bus pulled up outside, ready to take everyone to jail that couldn't pay their fines. My pulse hammered at the ominous sound of gravel crunching beneath those tires, and a chill crept up my neck. I thought with dread that there was a seat with my name on it. That was it—the threat of certain doom drove me to action. I *had* to get out of there fast. In one last desperate attempt to take control of my own fate, I called Brody, my former pimp, and assured him I was not running with the same people who had stolen his phone. I was sober now. He said I sounded good and guaranteed some work for me that night. *I can do this,* I thought, willing myself to believe.

But I was not out of danger yet. Sweating, I quickly told my dad that I had just been hired at a friend's company. If he could *please* take care of these fines, I could pay him back *very* soon. He relented and paid the fines in the nick of time. Sighing in relief, I was released minutes before I would have been recognized and most certainly locked up. But even more than relieved, I was now steeled in my resolve. This narrow escape convinced me I had to take back the reins of my life—whatever that might cost.

It was finally time for me to work. I told Max that I would start modeling. But I went to work the way I knew how, and I took some high-end clients, as my pimp called them. I also did some amateur porn shoots in Phoenix. After those jobs, the big offer finally came: the offer to become a real porn star. I thought, *Well, that beats wondering each night if someone will murder me in my hotel where no one ever finds me. At least with porn, if I die, there will be witnesses.* There it was—my thought process for why it made sense for me to make porn at this point in my life. One way or another, I thought death was the most likely outcome.

No matter how badly I hurt, I had to keep a smile on or at least a straight face.

Before I could move ahead into my new future, Brody ordered me to get used to violent sex. No matter how badly I hurt, I had to keep a smile on or at least a straight face. He tested me first. Then he sent me off to other directors in Los Angeles to do the same, only this time, on film. They didn't pay me for the movie, but at least I had a place to sleep. I was off to be sold to the bigger wolves. I no longer had to look over my shoulder for cops. My lifestyle was about to become legal, and porn would become a permanent reminder for the public's viewing of all the humiliation I had endured in my lifetime.

LITERALLY BURNED OUT

I had finally arrived. Hello, Los Angeles! The big giant letters *L-A-X* greeted me as I exited the airport. The city streets were jammed with luxury cars as their reflective surfaces glittered and glimmered in the sun. The fast pace and the ambitions swirled in the air. The Hollywood sign beckoned me from the mountainside near the beautiful tall Hustler building. I thought, *I'm no longer some street girl from Tucson. I am free to start my new life.* I breathed deeply, inhaling much more than oxygen as I was now the next Hollywood hopeful to channel strength and drive from this promise-filled atmosphere laced with lust for freedom and fame.

It was time to get busy. I stayed with a local producer and shot my first professional porn footage for free in exchange for rent. He and his roommates, who also performed, took me around to all the local production companies, where I took off all my clothes, let them snap a picture, showed them my ID, and waited for a call. I was sober and feeling good, and I was soon called back for video shoots. At one of the callbacks, I met my first official agent.

He had a mansion in Woodland Hills where he held Hollywood-style porn parties, and he invited me to live with him and four of his other girls. There was alcohol galore, which I justified as long as I did not get back into drugs. The drinks helped make filming a lot less painful—emotionally *and* physically. My agent rented out his house for shoots, so I could pick up work as soon as I got out of bed. When I wasn't filming, I helped out on set. I worked hard to make a name for myself in the business.

The girls he managed were flying off to Vegas for shows and being set up for private events with actors, producers, and any other big spender looking for a conquest for the night. He pimped us out on the side in addition to hosting the movie shoots, but since they took us out to nice dinners in fancy cars and introduced us to famous people, it didn't feel like the prostitution I was used to. I was making a significant amount of money each day and spent whatever I had left after the pimp and agent fees on more costumes—all so I could take more photos to get more work.

My initial plan was to stay two weeks and get out. I wanted to make enough to go back to school and not worry about having to work. But the money kept coming in and so did the attention. I couldn't help but chase after it once I had a taste. I got offers to work for the well-known names in the sex industry, and I felt I had arrived. I was shooting movies for premium cable channels and becoming involved in what I thought was the more glamorous side of the sex-selling business.

After a couple months, my new agent demanded more and more of me. I was a petite, blonde-haired, blue-eyed girl, so directors and agents wanted to set me up with the largest men and as many men as possible. A couple of weeks later, my body quit working. I was in pain all the time. I went to an adult-industry doctor who told me that I had acquired a second-degree chemical burn on my cervix because of the many products I had been using in order to perform as much as they needed me to. I was officially out of commission. Or so I thought. When I told the directors that I couldn't work, they told me to up the Xylocaine—a prescription cream to numb my parts. The other option they gave me was to start working with another area of my body.

In no time at all, my agent was well on his way to burning me out, typical in the industry. Agents set up their girls as quickly as possible with the most hardcore scenes to force them to push their limits. My agent said things like, "Nobody will want to use you in shoots anymore unless you keep taking it up a notch." I was now doing scenes that were more shocking. As the camera panned away from my face, I would bury my head in the pillow and cry. I cried whenever the camera was not facing my direction.

During one such shoot, one of the guys saw my tears and the way I flinched anytime he came close. He could tell I was in pain, and so he couldn't perform his job. My not-so-hidden sobs made him feel guilty. But this was not the time for anyone to grow a conscience. Instead, as a true professional, I had to pull it together and put all physical pain and emotional baggage aside for the moment. I reached deep down for the actress in me so we could finish the scene to the producer's approval. After all, three other actors, an agent, and a director were all counting on me to get paid. I did not want to make these men angry. I did whatever it took to ensure more work.

FROM PORN TO REHAB

The obsession to use drugs returned one day on set while trading detailed drug stories with the producer. His drug of choice was crack cocaine, and mine was meth. We talked about it so much that my physical cravings returned. (Discussing past drug use in detail can trigger a recovering addict's body to feel high again, which can possibly lead to a relapse.) By the time the shoot was over, I was on a mission to score. I was willing to go to any lengths to get it. I coerced my agent into having the limo driver take us into an area where the driver had some connections. Since we were rolling around town in a limo, no one found the clouds of smoke leaving the vehicle suspicious.

I introduced my agent to smoking meth along with some of the other ladies and gentlemen in the house. Soon all of us started to miss work, just sitting in the house, spun out of our minds on drugs. When the drugs were almost gone, we had a huge party with enough alcohol to reduce the effects of being up all week. A male performer who lived with us began to hit me up for sex. He called me obscene names until I finally let him do whatever he wanted to me. I did not want this guy to spread vicious rumors about me and possibly ruin my career, so I gave in with one condition: I could smoke the rest of my drugs first. Once again, I lay there as another man used me like a helpless, lifeless rag doll.

In an attempt to compensate for my disappointment in myself, I begin to invest in improving my image. If I looked good on the outside, then surely no one could tell how I died a little more each day on the inside. I picked out clothes and all sorts of finer accessories, and this new image made me feel as if my LA trip was a success. Even so, not far beneath the shallow sense of achievement, I needed something familiar and thought that it was time for me to return home. I still couldn't believe I had ended up high again and had taken a house full of people down with me. But I had. So I booked a plane to leave LA behind me.

Who else but Max, of course, picked me up from the airport. When he first saw me, I returned his gaze as he took in the new me. I now officially looked like I belonged on the cover of a hardcore porn magazine. Max was not happy with me, but I had a ton of money, so we went out and spent it on psychedelics for all his friends.

Max and I were barely speaking, but I faithfully left him money on the counter for whatever he needed, and so our living arrangement seemed to work fine. I was not home much; I was always taking off for more work so I could keep buying more drugs for everyone. And now that I had been to LA, Brody could raise my rate. My pimp promoted me in ads in the local papers and magazines with these words: "Get massaged by a porn star."

My pimp promoted me in ads in the local papers and magazines with these words: "Get massaged by a porn star."

One day, after working through the night, I came home in the morning to find our neighbor girl sitting in Max's lap, smoking weed. Never mind that *I* was out at all hours doing whatever, jealousy overcame me! I threw an entire case of soda at him and ran out of the house.

I roamed the streets, chasing with one gang after another. One day I would be with a certain gang, and the next day, I associated with their rivals. That could have led to serious trouble or even death. But I didn't care who I was with; all that mattered was that they had drugs. Then the inevitable happened. I ran out of money. I had no more drugs. The withdrawals began, and I once again lost control of my body. I no longer could speak, nor did I have any muscle control to open my hands. I found my way back to Max's house, and he and all the other guys just shook their heads, laughed, and called me names. They had lost all respect for me by this point. I went straight back to his room and called his dad.

His dad worked for the mental health department for the state of Arizona. I somehow screeched over the phone line that I needed help, and his dad told me how to get myself help for good. I gathered enough strength to ask Max to take me to a building called Sam Help. He willingly dropped me off there, comforted that he didn't have to worry about me any longer. He had done all he could for me. I was now the state's problem.

I was a bawling mess, embarrassed by my pathetic state. I walked into that unit, pulling at my hair and going out of my mind. I threatened, "If you guys don't help me get off these drugs, I'm going outside and walking in front of a bus!" They placed me in a private room and monitored me as I continued to lose my grip with reality. After what seemed like hours of hearing voices, they finally admitted me to the ER to detox. As I changed into my hospital gown, some drugs I had forgotten about fell out of my pocket. How could I have missed those? But no, I was done; I flushed them down the toilet before I could think twice about taking them.

The doctors hooked me up to all sorts of IVs and put me on a lot of medications to clear up the infections I had from work—infections that were running rampant in my body. I was evaluated by the state, and I told them my mental history prior to using drugs. I told them about my self-mutilating, attacks of paranoia, and personality disorders that came out in the middle of my rages. I told them about everything I had ever been diagnosed with since I was a little girl and about how I wanted to die. The state declared me seriously mentally ill (SMI) and admitted me to their custody, a psychiatric hospital, for thirty days.

In the facility, we couldn't have anything sharp, so I found other ways to harm myself until I finally stabilized. When I was deemed safe, I could have visitors. My dad was contacted, and he brought me comic books on his visits. He read them and explained them to me, because my brain was still slow to process information due to the drugs. He wanted to bring simplicity and joy back to my life and help me forget about this nightmare.

Eventually, I began to feel comfortable there. My medication, combined with a safe environment, helped me start interacting with people again. The men and women lived on separate floors, but we all got together to play bingo on Friday nights. I was learning how to actually have fun again, like the kind of fun I should have had as a child.

After my time in the psychiatric facility, I transitioned to a group home to wait for a bed to open up in the rehab center. At the group home, a male counselor began an affair with me. I didn't understand the ethical boundaries he was crossing, not to mention the illegality of his actions. I now wonder how many mentally unstable women he took advantage of beside me. Eventually, a bed opened up in rehab, and I moved out of that place, ending the affair. It was definitely for the best.

The rehab facility at Casa de Vida had two halls: one for addicts and one for those with a dual diagnosis of addiction and mental disorders. I was placed in the dual diagnosis unit. I learned how to work again by cooking and cleaning the facility. Then I focused on completing the assignments so that I could progress through recovery. I was back! By reading recovery books and concentrating on one sentence at a time, my brain became active again. I started reading my Bible, too, and eventually, they deemed me fit to transition to the other hall: the rehab unit for addicts. The timing was right since my roommate was telling me that she had murdered a family member, and I was starting to feel as if she didn't trust me. I now had a new roommate. But she wasn't any better. She convinced me to do sexual things with her, and I obliged, not wanting to upset her.

My dad came to visit me, and this time, he brought a woman, Becky. I was thrilled to see him seriously dating. I thought, *If he is bringing a woman to meet his daughter in rehab, this must be it for him.* He had not previously been serious about a woman because he knew his daughters would have two polar opposite reactions. I would instantly call her Mommy, and my sister would disown him for moving on. So he tried to wait until we turned eighteen. But this just led to secret or drunken affairs in his loneliness, and as I mentioned earlier, once I was old enough, they weren't so secret anymore.

This woman was amazing and supportive. I asked her if she planned on having kids with my dad, not realizing how inappropriate that was to ask during our first meeting. I was still learning proper social conduct. I didn't realize it yet, but this woman full of strength, grace, and compassion would be around for life.

After visiting hours, it was time for group. I had written out my life story and shared it in class. I was sure to include details, such as the names of the top producers I had worked for, because I was so proud of my past. My story enticed a young man at the facility who had previously made pornographic home movies. We became friends, and one night, while my new female roommate was away, he cut open the screen to my window and snuck in from outside. After he left, I thought we had gotten away with it, but apparently, he had done

90

this before with other girls at the rehab, friends of my roommate. These other, scorned women were lying in wait for an opportunity to seek revenge.

When my roommate returned, she found out what happened and flew into a jealous rage. At group, she confessed that she had used drugs while on her pass and was being kicked out. But in her jealousy, she didn't only tell on herself. She and the last girl he was with before me decided the group needed to know what I had done as well. But amazingly, in the consequences this set in motion, I wasn't alone. He cared enough to stand up for me and leave with me as the group voted me out of rehab. After six months of facilities, rehabs, and sobriety, I eventually had to leave because of the one addiction I just couldn't shake: men.

> *After six months of facilities, rehabs, and sobriety, I eventually had to leave because of the one addiction I just couldn't shake: men.*

After we were kicked out, I took a bus with this guy to his grandpa's home. We prepared to part ways; he was being sent back to prison to finish out his original sentence. He was only in rehab on the condition that he successfully completed the program, and since he did not finish treatment, he did not meet the conditions of his release. However, we still made plans for the future. In hopes of actually living out the future we had dreamed, I stayed sober, trying to make a life for us. I worked as many hours as I could at Coco's bakery. I found a small apartment for us, rode the bus to visit him every week, and wrote to him every day. He told me that when he got out, he would marry me. He also told me that I could be the stepmother to his children, including their fourth one that was now on the way.

RELAPSE

When he was released a couple months later, we immediately started drinking together in celebration and triumph. We were members of society again. Nothing would hold us back! He told me it was okay to drink because he was a crack addict and I was a meth addict, so alcohol was not the problem. Only I *was* a teenage alcoholic too. But I didn't know it at the time. I started fights with him, throwing punches like in the old days, and he hit me back—*hard*. He said that if I was going to fight like a man, I deserved to be hit like a man. We drank more and fought more.

The difference between us was that when we drank, he could stop, and I couldn't. I would become so intoxicated that I would force myself to throw up just so I could drink more. I thought this was normal behavior and left the bathroom door open as I did this. He pulled my hand out of my mouth and restrained me; then he locked me up in the bedroom until I calmed down.

Within weeks of living together, he left to attend the delivery of his fourth child. He planned to also get us a car and some cash. His baby momma was well off and well connected. He was miserable with how little we were living on, but I was ecstatic to be free and be with him. Oh, how I longed to be a wife, a member of a family, and a mom to this new baby. I wanted a normal life. It was honestly all I'd ever wanted since I was a little girl.

After one of the best workdays ever, I hopped on the bus and made my way home. A successful day was on the books, and I had a man of my very own to come home to. I opened the door to find everything of his gone. No note, no phone call, no nothing—just gone.

I laid there and sobbed. How could this be? I had done everything possible to be a homemaker. Was it because I'd cut my hair short? Because I dyed it too dark? Did he want me to look like a porn star? Three days later, he came back to apologize for returning to his family and his children, who, in all reality, fully deserved their father. He slept with me one more time, left me lying in bed, and went on his way.

I was popping open the fridge when in walked my dad's girlfriend, Becky. Sometimes, she showed up at Coco's and ate just to check in on me and let me know she was available to be my friend. This time, she came to my house because she knew I was struggling. Dad was out of town on business, and my future husband had disappeared. She seemed to know it was only a matter of time before I started to destroy my life again. She went straight to the fridge, dumped out all my alcohol, and took me out to eat at Chuy's. I was beginning to see her not only as a new mother figure in my life, but as someone I could truly consider a friend.

Unfortunately, her plan didn't work out. I had some downstairs neighbors who partied hard. They heard my wailing after the break up and offered me a bottle of Bacardi 151 to help ease my pain. I had been told both in rehab and at other meetings that I shouldn't date during my first year of sobriety. They were right. I was not strong enough to handle his return from prison without celebrating, and I was also not strong enough to handle the grief when he left. Both were a reason to drink alcohol in my mind.

But even so, I fought to maintain a hold on my new, reformed life, and so I went to a recovery meeting before I could spiral out of control. I even found a sponsor like they suggested, and I called her one night, completely trashed. She called me back the next day. "Oh, Deanna." Her voice dripped with pity. "You're supposed to call me *before* you pick up a drink."

My heartbeat slowed to a crawl, and all my best intentions shattered under the weight of her words. Then an all-too-familiar shame sunk its teeth into me, numbing me against the pain that always eventually came whenever I tried to change. Its poison spread outward like ice in my veins and continued reaching and reaching until it stopped and then froze my heart. *Oh, well. I tried, and I failed.*

Resignation echoed deep in my soul like the clamor of a prison cell door, deadening hope for a different life. With damaged relationships and failure at recovery, life with Brody seemed to be my only option. So I gave in to the negative charges I leveled at myself and pronounced my own sentence: I would follow Brody's next direction for my life and become whatever he wanted me to be.

CHAPTER TEN

UNCOVERING TIANA

As ALWAYS, Brody came to the rescue when I was at my lowest. He took me to some supposedly high-class, low-key alcohol lounges to find work, even though I was still under twenty-one. He advertised my pictures from the LA porn agency to some of the clientele at the bar, and after a few Long Island's and a bag of coke, I was ready to work for the weekend.

By Sunday afternoon, I found myself alone in a random guy's house, stewing in utter disgust at my own sorry state. I thought, *Why is this my life*? I watched my heart pulsating in my stomach as I came down from the weekend high. In one last desperate attempt to salvage whatever I could from it, I searched through a phone book and called a rehab center. But after I talked with a counselor, I backed out, claiming I wasn't ready. Immediately after I hung up, I dialed my friend Tia, who came to get me. She had the drugs I craved now that my pimp limited my drug use to cocaine. He told me that the incessant picking and rapid weight loss that came with crystal meth messed with my appearance, which negatively affected his sales.

Brody wasn't too upset when I returned to him high on meth, since I brought Tia with me to work for him too. He told us to pack our things, because we were going to Gilbert, Arizona, to shoot some amateur internet porn for the weekend. Drugs and alcohol on hand, I was ready to relaunch a career on camera. *At least filmed sex work means I won't have to see client after client for the next few days,* I thought. *Maybe I'm of some value to someone—even if it is a pimp and a porn producer.*

I worked on the film with a nice guy named Andy. Because of my deeply entrenched addiction, once we finished shooting that weekend, I, of course, went off the rails on a drug binge. I started fights with girls at strip clubs and passed out at another stranger's house in a city I knew nothing about. Andy eventually found me and brought me to his home. He told me he really liked me and wanted me to clean up. I could hardly believe it: Here was a man selling his own body for sex, and he wanted to be the one who rescued *me* from this life.

> *I dreamed of a future that could turn the nobody I felt like I was into a somebody, important and famous.*

But Tia had other plans in mind for us. She wanted to try the big leagues. I told her that with Brody's permission, I could introduce her to some of the producers I knew in California. I took off from Andy's with both his heart and his finest bottle of Jack Daniel's—arriving in LA, intoxicated by alcohol and the hope of a better future. I dreamed of a future that could turn the nobody I felt like I was into a somebody, important and famous.

A new agent met us at the airport. My last agent had apparently gotten hooked on the drugs I'd introduced him to. Fortunately for him, though, he went to jail, came out, and found both God and a better way of living. I had no such luck. I was back to what I considered to be my stepping stone to fame, which was legal prostitution and the creation of self-degrading materials that would never go away. But here I was, just the same. My new agent waited for us to sober up for a day or so before agreeing to take us through the usual routine of taking photos in front of producer after producer. After putting all of ourselves out there, we went back to the hotel to wait for a call.

IN DEMAND

I had learned my lesson from the first time I was in LA, so I told my new agent that I only wanted to work with certain males and would absolutely not partake in the outrageous and violent scenes my last agent had expected. I had no idea I could demand the kind of work I wanted, but when I did, I gained some control over my body. It was as if I had a small voice in who I would be sold to that day.

I was booked with plenty of work, but that same week, I found out the shocking and humiliating news that both Tia and I had an STD. I couldn't work until I took my antibiotics and my test came back negative. This was a common occurrence in the industry, usually resolved in a week or so. But with an unexpected week to kill and the money we had left over from our work in Arizona, I called my former limo driver, and he brought us some drugs. We used antibiotics and meth to help lessen the pain and embarrassment from our STDs.

The antibiotics worked, and I was called to come in for shoots. Since STDs were frequent in our line of work, I now had antibiotics on hand all the time. If I was worried, I could take them before my next mandatory STD test was scheduled a mere thirty days later. In this industry, you could always find a way to medicate—nothing interrupted my work for long.

In addition to maintaining my physical health, I also had a ritual to take care of my mental health as I gave myself over to publicly watched and owned sex work. An hour before the shoot, I chugged a forty of Old English beer. I kept another in my costume bags in one of my shoe boxes for when that wore off. After this routine, I showed up to the set where I was scheduled with all the liquid courage I needed to make it through the day's demands.

One day, while working on a new set, I crossed paths with the people who would change the course of my career. As I was trying on the different outfits available for his movie, the producer offered me some Grey Goose—or anything else I desired from his fine alcohol collection, which was pristinely displayed like a trophy case. This display was next to another trophy case, which was filled with awards for his movies. Relieved that drinking was acceptable to him, I pulled the forty of beer out of my shoebox and said, "Thanks, I brought my own."

He laughed at my cheap bottle and clearly alcoholic behavior and said, "Carry on." I got along well not only with the producer, but also with the star of his movie—so well that, after working together, she and I became an inseparable pair. She invited me to live in her house since I had been staying in a hotel. I originally thought my visit to LA would be temporary, but at this point, I thought, *Let's see where this goes.* I was once again back in Woodland Hills in an extravagant house, and I left Tia behind—who instead preferred to go home and do drugs with her friends anyway. Now that I was living with my new friend, Cassie, I got to party with the top porn stars as well as with other mainstream actors and musicians who popped in for porn-star karaoke and after-parties.

Through Cassie's connections, I started getting nude magazine work, which required me to seriously sober up, at least long enough to shoot still photographs. Then, one week before a photoshoot with a famous photographer, I felt a lump the size of a large golf ball in my breast. *Did this just appear? Was I so high I never noticed it before?*

I rushed to the ER where I cried by myself in the hospital bed with no family or friends to support me. The doctors poked needles in and out of my enlarged breast to drain any fluid. The lump turned out to be a cyst and not an infection or anything more sinister. But with an expensive ER bill, I definitely couldn't afford to lose any work.

I pushed ahead with my schedule but was mortified when I had to show up to the set of this internationally respected and well-known photographer the next week with my breast discolored green, black, and blue from the testing. The make-up artist was unconcerned, however, and went to work. After a little airbrushing to cover up the discoloration as well as my other scars and marks from previous years of cutting, I was ready for wardrobe.

From then on, I was booked for what I perceived as high-end sex-industry work. I worked in television, print, and even late-night radio shows, where I was interviewed beside a famous rapper. My pay continually increased, and so did my recognition. Professionally, I changed my name to "Tiana." That's who the world really wanted. Each time I was recognized in public, a little part of Deanna died. Our culture had progressed so much sexually that people continually admitted to paying money to stores, which paid money to producers, who paid money to purchase me—and resell me. Forever. Some people used porn so often, they not only recognized me but also had no shame in asking for my autograph when they saw me in public. Curious and confusing though it all was, in my most sober moments, my work was now recognized, and the fame was intoxicating—so the career seemed legitimate to me.

I stayed longer in LA this time and soaked up the new lifestyle. The couple I lived with was well known in the sex industry. I officially belonged to them—for whatever ways they wanted to amuse themselves—and we traded any connections we came across. We all went to swingers clubs, a common expression of open sexuality in LA among married couples. But somehow, I took even these experiences too far. How do you take it too far at a swingers club? Time after time, I had to be locked up in my room again so I could calm down from my publicly underage alcohol rages On the one hand, I was progressing in my career, but I was also still locked up in the cages of my many addictions.

> *Our culture had progressed so much sexually that people continually admitted to paying money to stores, which paid money to producers, who paid money to purchase me —and resell me. Forever.*

NO MORE DRUGS

On Memorial Day weekend 2004, I had been doing coke for so many days, I honestly could not feel my face anymore. Coke was the socially acceptable drug of the porn industry, so I had finally switched to it. In fact, my limo driver had even become the official supplier of the household and joined in on the parties. We spent thousands of dollars on food for our parties and even more on drugs. But once we started using the drugs, no one ate the food.

On this particular holiday weekend, I had used so much coke that my nose swelled shut. I was unable to breathe and in excruciating pain, so I went to the guest house on the property to come down off the drugs. My friend who lived there knew that I had been trying and struggling to avoid using again. Before this party began, I'd had about ten days of sobriety under my belt. I'd ignored this friend's warning when I had one dirty martini at the beginning of the party, which left me craving the hard drugs. Now truly in pain and remorseful, I was lying on his couch, trying to do all I could to just breathe again through my nostrils and fall asleep for even a little bit. I tried to calm myself down for hours before I finally managed to drift off to sleep.

My agent picked me up the next morning and asked if I was going to do my hair. They didn't have makeup on location that day. "My hair is done!" I announced dismissively. He rolled his eyes at my pathetic state and drove toward the day's location. I had just happened to get booked for what was considered one of the top feature companies in the business. I would not make a great first impression with my disheveled appearance.

Somehow, the producer was okay with how I looked and was happy with how the scene went anyway. One of his main contract girls also used cocaine, so he was familiar with it. He was a cool guy and offered to take me out to eat and talk shop. We went out for tacos, and after he shared some pointers of the business, I realized with sudden and intense clarity that I could finally become a star if I cleaned up for good. I don't remember much else from the conversation, but a switch seemed to flip inside me at the possibility of stardom. He seemed to do well for himself and so did the girls who worked for him, so I hungrily took his advice.

I had a serious talk with my agent, moved out of Cassie's house, and lived in a hotel for the next six months. If I was going to stay clean, I needed to be away from all influences of drugs. I kept busy and went for walks down Ventura Boulevard in my bikini top with music blaring from my headphones. I went into Petco and fed raisins to the chinchillas almost every day. When I engaged with the friendly little mammals, this helped me feel connected to life. This was better than being strung out of my mind. I also stayed accountable to my agent, my pimp, and the agency manager. Once and for all, I was going to do this business right and follow a clear path, and I was getting enough work that I could afford living at the Extended Stay. Each room had its own kitchen, which felt like a small luxury. Living alone and responsibly was an achievement on my journey to cleaning up *for* and moving up *within* the professional porn industry. My career goals motivated me, so I confidently moved into my next phase of freedom, sure that I had arrived. Who knew that a concrete career goal, rather than the ambiguous promise of a better life, would finally help me get clean?

Even though I couldn't quit drugs as Deanna, I discovered that I could as Tiana. And so Tiana became my new identity, my new life. I would do anything to help keep that name and the powerful, successful gig attached to it going.

CHAPTER ELEVEN

MY PUBLIC AND FOREIGN AFFAIRS AT TWENTY-ONE

THOUGH I HAD FINALLY found a way to kick *hard* drugs, getting clean and growing in fame were both a process for me. On one hand, my career was continuing its upscale climb in the sex industry, and these films were being nominated for globally recognized awards. I now had my own videos that featured anyone else I wanted to. I spent afternoons signing autographs at porn stores and got my foot in the door of some major, well-known, multi-million dollar contract companies. But on the other hand, as my popularity increased, so did my drinking. Not even twenty-one yet and still clueless I was an alcoholic, I was now drinking alcohol behind the scenes while waiting for the other talent to finish with makeup. Production managers had warned others of my drinking problem. But I thought nothing of sneaking off to drink cooking wine from the kitchen staff on location. After all, drinking cooking wine wasn't any crazier than being filmed having sex with a stranger to feed other people's addictions.

While in the dressing room one day, I overheard a phone call to the director from a medical clinic that served professional sex workers. The call changed everything for our shoot. After only a half day of filming, all production had to stop immediately. The industry was put on quarantine, and an antibiotic was not going to fix this problem. A performer who had recently come back from Brazil had transmitted HIV to some others in the biz.

The industry had three levels of quarantine: quarantine of the immediate actors involved, quarantine of the actors who had worked with the immediate actors, and finally, a quarantine of those actors who had worked with the second tier of actors. Startled, I realized how easily my name could have been on one of those lists. But by the grace of God, I was not part of this or any other quarantine while I was in the porn industry. Though this particular experience was a huge eye-opener for me, in the end, not even a fatal disease scare could stop me from working. And so as I left this set, I moved on to new projects—and to new relationships.

> *The industry was put on quarantine, and an antibiotic was not going to fix this problem.*

I moved from my tiny room at the Extended Stay into a real apartment with another up-and-coming performer named Danni, who was also drug-free. She showed me how to enjoy life—going out to eat, shopping, going to the movies, going swimming, hanging out with people our age, and more—when I wasn't performing. The problem with all this was that I had no idea how to separate my on-camera character from my real self. I was used to being at upscale places with high-end people who knew other industry people, so entertainment of every sort was acceptable to me. I had learned that when money and status were at your disposal, anything illegal was somehow conveniently overlooked.

Since this mentality was deeply ingrained within me, I often embarrassed my roommate. I took my performances at our home parties too far and caused fights on a nightly basis. In addition, I was also very open about my life in the porn industry while Danni was instead trying to live and lead a double life—and teach me how to do the same. She lied about what she did to her boyfriends, her friends, and her family. She even tried to cover up the fact that she was still seeing her ex despite his possessive and controlling behavior. Even though she looked pristine on the outside, she was involved in the drama too. This friendship turned out to be dysfunctional as well.

But who needed normal friends when I had people accessible for my every whim? I had drivers to take me wherever I wanted to go, and nearly everything I wanted was delivered to me. A manicurist even came over to do my nails at home. She actually preferred doing them when I was passed out from alcohol, because it was easier than when I was trembling from alcohol withdrawals, anxious, or fidgety. She came in, put a hundred dollars' worth of rhinestones on my fake nails, and left with a couple hundred bucks for her service. I paid top dollar to maintain my image.

TWENTY-ONE

On the night of my twenty-first birthday, Danni and I walked to the store at midnight to buy the seven hundred dollars' worth of liquor we planned to drink that night. After a few drinks, I began to chase my next fatal inappropriate attraction, but he wasn't paying any attention to me. He left the party, and after a few more drinks, I went looking for him. I walked by the neighbor's open apartment door and saw him sitting next to a girl on a couch. In that moment, I was overwhelmed with rage. I punched her, grabbed him, and set out to prove I was worth his attention.

My adventures that night weren't over after this conquest, though. I still had more to prove. Still desperate to build a real friendship with Danni, I went to hunt down a girl who was running her mouth about my roommate. I found this girl at a local gym and cornered her against her car. I eventually let her go, but then she came back through our neighborhood and started shouting. I went upstairs to grab a fork to use as a weapon, and I started running around the complex, intent on hurting her. Someone called the cops, and before I knew it, I had hit the officer in the face. Until then, it had all been fun and games. But suddenly, my freedom and a possible felony were on the line.

Amazingly, Danni came to my rescue and diffused the situation. She talked the cop into letting me go because I wasn't taking my mental health medication.

I had been prescribed at least eight pills, including anti-depressants, anti-psychotics, and mood-stabilizing medications.

Despite the near jail experience and the fact that I was already clearly out of control, I continued drinking as the night wore on. By now, my roommate was fed up with my drama. Unaware of this, my behavior escalated, and I went streaking around the apartment complex. Remember, my roommate was still trying to maintain some dignity, so I crossed a new line with this escapade. I sought sympathy from a friend of hers, who unbeknownst to me, was actually her frightening ex. She had introduced me to him under a different name, so I had no idea who he really was or that she was still pursuing him. As we were headed back to his place, she started blowing up his phone with jealous texts. When I returned, she was yelling at me and finally told me who his real name. After more yelling, I went to punch her in the face, missed, and punched a hole in her bathroom door instead. That was the final straw, and I was out of there for good.

Four large guys managed to restrain me and take me into the other bathroom where they barricaded me until I sobered up. Within minutes, I started breaking things and cutting myself. I needed to release the deep shame that overwhelmed me. Eventually, I passed out, and I awoke the next morning to the all-too-familiar scene of bloody towels. This same scene still haunted my memories of childhood, but I never imagined I would take these memories with me from Arizona to California.

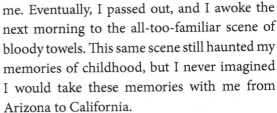

That was the last time, on the dawn of my twenty-first year, that I would cut myself.

Everyone was shocked at my actions, including myself. I could not believe this behavior had followed me into my new life. I looked at myself in the bathroom mirror and blinked slowly. I tried to see the face before me and not my mother—not all the blood on our fancy decorative guest towels. As I tried to focus on my own image, disbelief and shame stared back at me and awakened a desire deep within. Somehow, this seemed stronger than the impulse to self-harm. *Each time I do this, it leaves scars and reminds me of the pain. I can't help it if others hurt me. But I can stop adding to these scars.* And I was right; something did change that night. That was the last time, on the dawn of my twenty-first year, that I would cut myself.

My drinking was embarrassing the agency, and industry writers were documenting my behavior. My annoyed agent picked me up that morning, but he reminded me that if I could get my act together, I could still see a successful future. I had two choices for my next career move: an offer to be on the Howard Stern show and another offer to sign autographs in Berlin, Germany, with the company who had given me my own series. I was deathly terrified of Howard Stern, because even though he would provide me with publicity, I was aware of his harsh reputation. I was afraid he would ask me about my past life before porn, which was all an ominous blur to me. I had yet to deal with the trauma from that time. I was not willing to open myself up to possible public ridicule. This decision was a no-brainer—I chose Berlin.

Berlin held the annual Venus awards show, also known as the Oscars of the Erotic Industry. The company I represented was up for Best Movie internationally. The rest of the U.S.- nominated performers and directors, who were all incredibly proud of their latest work, also attended.

With sixteen hours to kill before the main event, we amused ourselves with giant bottles of liquor we bought at the duty-free store. Despite my intentions to straighten out, alcohol was too much a part of me to hold back now. I purchased a large bottle of Malibu, the same drink my pimp used to give me to relax me before work. I drank most of it before I got on the plane. Even though we were obnoxious and completely plastered, we were still recognized as industry professionals, so we got away with atrocious behavior with no regard for the civilians on the plane.

We made it to Berlin, but my immune system was shot by that point, so I couldn't handle the recycled air of such a long flight. I developed an extremely high fever overnight, but missing work was not an option. My company had flown me to Berlin for only one reason: to get publicity for them. I drank to numb the symptoms of my illness so that I could show up and perform live for the crowds. The regulations for European sex-trade shows were much less strict than those in the United States. What I had become accustomed to at home was much worse in Germany. I needed a lot of liquid courage for what I learned was expected of me, so naturally, I drank excessively.

By the time I returned to the hotel, I was begging for crack to sober me up. At the end of the four-day show and after many unsuccessful attempts to acquire drugs, I surrendered to the endless special award-show drinks instead, and I was intoxicated enough to leave the party all together. I still had not touched drugs since the previous Memorial Day weekend, and I was proud of that accomplishment. Even so, when I drank, the sense of pride was far from my mind, and I tried to get my hands on drugs many times. Somehow, and maybe even miraculously, I always passed out from alcohol before I could connect with anyone I was randomly dialing in my oblivion.

If I had been successful in my frantic search for drugs, it would have cost me my life. But instead, I had taken off, roaming the streets of a foreign country where I didn't even speak the language. The owner of the company I was representing had no idea where I'd gone, and neither did I. I came rolling in by night's end with a homeless guy on my arm. One of the dominatrix performers who was with our group yanked this guy off me and sent him on his way.

I was furious. "How dare you try to control me?" I then punched the owner of the company in the face. He was large, Italian, intimidating, and reminded me of a character from *The Sopranos*. He said, slowly and menacingly, "Don't you *ever* do that again." You would think that his demeanor alone would have stopped me, but no. *Bam!* I punched him again. Finally, after the third punch, he picked me up by my throat so forcefully that I had four huge bruises in the shape of his fingerprints on my neck the next day. I ran out of the room crying, not understanding why everyone was mad at me. My boss left the country without me. I was just thankful he did not cancel my ticket home.

PUBLIC SCRUTINY

Once I came home, I was horrified that my behavior was so excessive, even for one of the world's wildest parties. I began to seriously work toward getting my act together. I went to the adult industry medical professionals to make sure I was clear to begin work again in the United States, and I also checked to see if my previous drug use had caused any unknown serious physical damage. I asked to be tested for Hepatitis C. I knew that my drug-related irresponsibility increased my risk of infection. And sure enough, the first test came back positive.

My life is over! Over! I can't leave my hotel, I thought, completely mortified. I somehow found enough strength to do the second set of tests, however, and these clarified that I officially did *not* have Hepatitis C. Even so, industry reporters had already gained wind of news about my supposed infection through other performers. After the rumors hit the internet, industry news professionals started calling my agent. With this latest development, he was done with me. I was too much of a hazard for his business. Drinking and starting fights was one thing, but now that I was a possible health liability, he would no longer represent me.

My doctor left me a message, clarifying I had no virus to transmit. But by then I had already confessed to the entire industry that I tested positive for Hep C even though I didn't actually carry the disease. I had to change my cell number after multiple reporters called. Everything I said to defend myself in interviews only made me sound worse. My only response was, "Yes, I was exposed to the virus, but no, I do not have it." All reporters heard was my confession. I did not have to disclose this in the porn industry, but I felt better letting everyone know up front what they were working with.

I was ridiculed so publicly on adult media forums that even the Centers for Disease Control took note and stepped in to explain cases like mine. The lead doctor with the adult industry medical facility followed with a public statement that she was astonished at the way media attention had turned into what she could only describe as a "witch hunt." Top gastroenterologists in the country also officially confirmed: I did *not* have Hep C.

While this media storm was raging around me and I was still hiding out in my hotel, the same company called me that had taken me to Berlin. They were going to be shooting some films in Prague since the sex-industry workers there were cheaper, and foreign DVD sales were strong. The performer they were originally bringing to Europe was not available, supposedly due to mouth surgery, which was probably another way of saying drug use. In any case, I was ready to prove to them that I would not be a liability. I had learned from the error of my ways.

The owner of this company needed some assurance that I could handle a project like this. He took me out to a bar in Los Angeles and asked me to show him that I was wild enough to take out of the country and could handle filming some of the things he was requiring. Desperate to prove myself, I mentally stepped into character and did whatever he asked the rest of the evening, no matter how humiliating it was to me. I was twenty-one, and he was in his fifties, so my compliance did much to show the watching world in the room how powerful he was. When we finally left, he took me back to his hotel and asked me to finish the job.

Desperate to prove myself, I mentally stepped into character and did whatever he asked the rest of the evening, no matter how humiliating it was to me

A NEW PLAN

After I proved myself capable of the trip, I landed in Prague. I couldn't believe the sights. Such culture, beauty, and rich history awaited me as I arrived in Europe, via the best first-class experience on Swiss Air. Thankful I did not get sick this time on the flight, I stepped out of the airport and took a deep, steadying breath. Even the air smelled cleaner in Europe. Blocking how I had earned such an experience, I drank in the magnificent views. I was filled with calm and wonder as we took a ride through the country to reach the exquisite apartment we would use during our time there. The tension and embarrassment I'd been living in drained out of me as a smile of relief and contentment spread across my face. The newness of the environment held a sweet and inviting promise, which reignited within me hope and resolve for moving forward.

Unfortunately, however, while I soaked in the beauty of this European escape, life in the States remained ugly for me. At home, the public scrutiny did not stop when I left. In fact, more rumors circulated online because I left the country with a supposed disease. Dreading the day I had to return, I spent about six weeks in Europe, focusing my attention on the jobs I did have and offering my personal best on and off camera. When I wasn't in a scene, I paid attention to the new girls who had been freshly scouted into the industry as they sat in the make-up chair, scared of what would be required of them. Despite the language barrier, I comforted them in hopes I would prove to be an asset to the company who had hired me. I was pleased with my own efforts and began to feel that both my camera performances and my off-camera professionalism showed that I was worth the ticket this time.

Now that I finally had my act together, I also had a plan. I would make a ton of money from all the scenes I was shooting, take it all back to Tucson, buy a car, rent an apartment, find a normal job, and be done with the industry for good. I had, after all, only wanted to be in the industry for a couple of weeks in the first place. How had I been trapped in this lifestyle for three years already?

After my continued hard work as a production assistant and a performer, working between one and three scenes a day, I proved myself indispensable to the company. A week before it was time to go back to the United States, I woke up to a pleased owner and two directors standing around my bed with drinks and cigars in hand. *Why are these men hovering over my bed, and why do they look so happy?* I wondered.

My sleepy eyes opened, and I rolled over, suddenly aware of the men surrounding my bed. The group acted like a bunch of giddy school girls. Then the owner grinned. "We have decided we won't let you go back to Arizona. If you want a real job, you've got it! You can start by helping out in the office on days that you aren't shooting. You're worth it, kid. You have gone above and beyond what any performer would do. You have helped us on every set, whether or not you were in the shoot. We like your character. We like who you are becoming. You can start when we get back to the United States." A warm rush of pride and delight mixed together inside me as the invitation sunk in.

111

"Are you serious?" I asked, nearly breathless. I was beyond thrilled.

They had made the decision for me: I was not going back to Arizona. They were not afraid of the press I would bring them since they had a long-standing reputation they were proud of. In fact, they were willing to bring me up under their name and give me a new exclusive series. My well-meaning intentions for leaving the industry quickly fell to the wayside. This powerful company had come up with a different plan for my life, and it was much better than my current lifestyle, living in some temporary hotel and waiting for work. Truth be told, I saw a quick ticket to financial freedom and independence with their plan. In Arizona, I'd have to struggle to make a new way of life, and I risked running into some of my past connections. There, I'd have to build a kind of normalcy I'd never known from the ground up. I wasn't sure that I could pull that off.

CHAPTER TWELVE

MOVING UP IN THE INDUSTRY

THE EXCITEMENT had not worn off. Now, as I lay snuggled in my covers remembering, I could hardly believe it: I had a chance to be something more than a porn performer. I could be appreciated for more than just my body. *I knew there was a reason that I graduated from high school early*, I thought. *Everything is falling back into place.*

The owner went home early to be with his family, but I stayed behind with the rest of the directors. Though a real job was now waiting for me, I was not yet finished with my role in Prague. The directors and I went out drinking to celebrate my new role and also to relax me for my next scene, especially since the European performer I was about to work with was very rough with women. I had set a hard line against doing such violent scenes when I first came back, but this scene was for a company that I now trusted. I was the cover girl for their critically acclaimed, multi-award-winning series. This was my next step to success, so I had to do whatever was necessary. Czech beer was on tap, flowing through the sink faucet in our apartment. I could drink as much as I needed to in order to check out mentally and physically. I came stumbling onto the set in my stilettos, ready to film.

I was so hammered that I was barely responsive in the shoot, so it looked more

113

like a helpless rape scene instead of the scene they had choreographed. They canceled the whole shoot and put me to bed. I didn't understand why everyone was so upset. I had given them all of my body. But they said the scene would have portrayed the actor taking advantage of me since I was barely conscious.

They called my boss, the producer. "Look guys, she's terrified," he said. "We'll reshoot that scene when you come back. I need to be there, or my director will have her filming for hours, and she will never want to work again. I'll be the director of that scene. She trusts me."

I woke up with horrible shakes the next morning. Normally, I fought those with another drink. But now, our agent in the Czech Republic stipulated that I was not allowed to drink if she was going to keep supplying us with talent. The last actor had gone home without a full paycheck, which was my fault, since I didn't finish performing the scene he showed up for. This new restriction reminded me I couldn't waste people's time and money. But what would I do to cope? *How am I going to calm down without a drink? Okay,* I told myself. *Breathe. Let's just get into makeup and see how I feel in two hours.*

Once, my back went out on set, and instead of stopping, the director told me to stay put and finish the scene.

The footage was rolling, and I began crawling on the table to tease the camera. But all I wanted to do was go back to bed. What *could* I do? My body was aching and throbbing; it hurt to walk. It hurt to even sit. I *needed* a drink! *Just keep crawling. Now walk over to the bar, flirt with the bartender, and order a shot.* Yes! I had just made alcohol part of the scene. I took a few shots, enough to calm my nerves, and then I was ready to go.

After wrapping up that scene, I decided not to film while detoxing again. I made a pact with our director that if he would sneak me beers, I would give him the Vicodin I'd been prescribed for my back problems, which were aggravated by what directors required the male performers to do to me. Once, my back went out on set, and instead of stopping, the director told me to stay put and finish the scene. I usually took only enough Vicodin to deal with the pain and traded the rest for something else I preferred. This week, I needed alcohol—not pain pills—to work. I finished out the week by filming under a controlled buzz.

CLOSE CALL

Finally, it was a wrap! Somehow I had made it through the last week, and now it was time to celebrate the close of filming five movies in five weeks. We were off to the bar. Driven by the relief and the insatiable thirst of an alcoholic, I happily caught the B-52s they set on fire and slid my way. After a few drinks, I caught the eye of some rugby players at the local pub. Now everyone there was really getting excited. Everyone, that is, except the people I'd come with. They rushed me out of there, warning me that I could have gotten them killed and myself abducted. After all, they were two normal-sized guys who had taken the entertainment away from big, drunk, salivating, sex-hungry men.

But what do you know—their method of calming me down was to bring me to my next bar, which was conveniently located at our stunning five-star hotel for the night. Eventually, the bartender cut me off. But that didn't stop me. I stumbled over to the nearest table and drank whatever leftover alcohol I could find. Finally, bar security came and escorted me up the steps. I was locked in my room, and in my intoxicated rage, I began to rip out the TV, phones, and everything else from the wall. Fortunately, I passed out before I could do any further damage.

When I woke up the next morning, I thought, *Oh no, I've done it again. I won't have a job when I get back.* My boss's reaction surprised me, though. He assured me over the phone that all would be fine.

He explained to the production crew, "Listen, Deanna is scared and acting out. She has no idea how to accept the possibility of success, and subconsciously, she is trying to throw it all away before it gets taken from her."

What? Could this be true? I wondered, as I pondered his analysis of me. *Is that what I have always done?* How was it that, after spending only one month with me, this man had figured out a key to my dysfunction? That was more insight than a lifetime of therapy and counselors had unearthed.

GOING TO WORK

On the Monday after we landed back in the United States, I didn't wait for a ride from my hotel to the office. This was my chance—my chance to prove to others in this industry that I was more than a body for purchase. I took a cab and was the first one there. I knew I had ambition, traits, and talents that could benefit a business. Upon my arrival, I discovered my job role was still undefined, but I was unfazed and started organizing files. My co-workers were all telling me, "Deanna, stop it. You have done more today than most of us do in a year."

I continued to apply this work ethic, and I started to feel alive again. I became so attached to the company and the people working there that I decided, with the owner, to contract with them. I would exclusively film for them and shoot four times a month but spend the rest of my time in the office. The more my bosses saw how hard I worked, the more perks I received. They helped me find and pay for an apartment and a car. I had a therapist and a personal trainer, and my company paid for classes at the community college, both general and health-related. I no longer had to go to the lab to be tested for STDs every few weeks because doctors came to the office instead. Yes, *this* was my new life!

Within a year, I was promoted from basic office administration to video-on-demand management, then from public relations to legal areas with documentation. Additionally, I served in the role of company representative in matters such as lobbying for freedom in porn at the state capitol. Most of the senators we sat down with for meetings had no stance against pornography whatsoever. At the time, I campaigned with pride for an industry whose people I cared about and within which I had experienced my own rise to fame. But even though I used the word "empowering" to describe what I was doing, that couldn't have been further the truth. Being sold through the legal porn industry was a sorry excuse for empowerment and hardly an escape at all from the life of prostitution I had so longed to leave behind. But it would take more time for me to see the truth of my own journey—and the truth about the porn industry—with clarity. For now, I focused on being a hard worker, committed to excelling at my job.

My self-confidence increased due to the reality of new and seemingly purposeful work in my life. With this, my need for alcohol seemed to decrease. In fact, I only drank occasionally now. Sometimes I had a few beers on a lunch break. Other times, I drank a bottle of champagne before a shoot or during the parties my co-workers and I had to attend in our line of work. Aside from a couple of occasions when my bosses found me passed out in the office the morning after I partied too hard the night before, I seemed to be managing my drinking fairly well. For a time, at least.

MY LAST SCENE

As my life continued to stabilize, I began to feel a stirring of something new inside me in January 2006, of all places, I was at the Adult Video News Convention in Las Vegas. This was going to be my year. In addition to being nominated for awards, I was asked to present awards that year, which was a huge honor.

Despite the surface glitz and glamor, every year, when I came home from these events, I had a mental, emotional, and spiritual breakdown. I had to stuff everything Deanna felt deep within me in order to become Tiana for four days straight. Everyone and everything came to this convention, which determined the worth of everything I'd done over the last year. I had never been more invested in the results than I was this year as both a presenter and a nominee.

But this year, I felt a pull between my professional attitude and my character, a tug-of-war, if you will. It was my first year as a contract girl and my first year building professional relationships behind the scenes. I was playing two very different roles all weekend, and it was dizzying. I was alternating between meeting new online distributors who could become potential clients and doing interviews with magazines back at the hotel. My contract stated that I would represent our company as their main girl.

I was asked about God in many of my interviews. I didn't know where the strength of my faith came from, but I was very confident of one thing: Jesus died for *me* too. That answer didn't go over well. The interviewers published magazines with me on the cover as the "Christian slut." I was so confused. I had

117

tried to be sincere, but they exploited it. I don't know why I expected anything different. At this point, I started praying to God, "Please, pleeeease, let me know when I'm done with this stage of my life!"

• • • • • • • • • • ◇ • • • • • • • • • • • •

I didn't know where the strength of my faith came from, but I was very confident of one thing: Jesus died for me too.

• • • • • • • • • • ◇ • • • • • • • • • • • •

Around this time, I began shooting photos regularly with an amazing photographer who shot a lot of actresses and singers on a daily basis, but I couldn't put all of myself into it. Here I was, working with this incredibly talented photographer right when I'd reached the point of not wanting to take naked photos anymore. I hated my body. I hated people looking at me.

A couple weeks after returning from Vegas, I was scheduled to shoot the fourth video in my series and perform in another one of the company's video series I was known for. At the same time, I happened to also be standing in as their national sales manager, which had been a rotating position for the past year. Exhausted after a typical eight-hour day at the office, I checked out mentally and showed up in the make-up chair, ready to switch characters and roles from Deanna to Tiana.

I had scheduled myself to work with two cool, down-to-earth, submissive porn actors because I needed an easy day. One of them was a vet who struggled with PTSD, and this was the only kind of work he could find. We all knew what to do because we'd worked together many times. Before the camera turned on, one of the performers was whispering kind things in my ear to relax me for our scene. "If I wasn't married, I'd want you to be my wife."

The new thing that had been stirring in me erupted in a sudden burst of clarity and hope—and deep, deep desire. I thought of him and his wife and how I wanted a relationship of my own. I wanted to go out on a date. I wanted to hear all these nice things and know that they were coming from someone who sincerely cared for me. I wanted to wake up next to someone and not receive a paycheck for it. But most of all, I wanted to put some clothes on.

"Stop the shoot!" I suddenly demanded.

I looked the director in the eyes with tears streaming down my cheeks, and with all the seriousness I could muster, I said, "I think I'm done performing."

We talked it through. I finished out my scene and offered to do things that I wouldn't normally do, mainly to market the video as my last recorded performance. I might have been naked in character as Tiana for the moment, but I was also still thinking about sales for the company—the company that had helped me realize a love for real work again.

I went home and told my roommate I was done. I knew I would lose a lot of money. But I was willing to risk it if I could finally be free from the testing, the antibiotics, the whole charade. I was incredibly nervous, though, because I still had another four months left on my contract. But a small voice inside told me if I gave up the contract, I would be okay. Sure enough, my boss did not seem surprised. I didn't know how he knew me so well, but he saw it coming. He told me he had stopped seeing me as Tiana for a while. Even though I would put on one outfit to take pictures with the public and then put on slacks and a blouse for our sales meetings, he could tell that I mentally and emotionally came to life in the office. Ultimately, he wanted to see me succeed.

He shared that he used to help all sorts of talent get off drugs and give them a chance to earn a living outside of performing, but he always watched the people he had come to care about revert back to their old ways. Well, not me. He told me he saw someone in me who was emotionally invested, who had taken in everything he had to teach her about life and business and had run with it. Eventually, I had even run all the way.

I was filled with awe at his words, but then a sobering question entered my mind. "What about my salary?

"Keep it, kid. I think you'll be worth every penny as a saleswoman."

The warmth I had started to recognize as self-worth spread out far and deep, like the roots of a well-watered tree. Hope radiated through my chest. I was finally done! All because someone had faith in me and in what I had to offer beyond my sexual capabilities.

Dear Diary,

January 22, 2006: I'm finally done with the camera! This time for good.

CHAPTER THIRTEEN

THE GRAVE EFFECTS OF PORN

RING. *RING.* "All right! Time to get busy!" I announced to myself in a contented, sing-song voice.

Orders were being processed. I was testing some new marketing techniques, and I thought enthusiastically, *It's going to be a great day!*

A voice interrupted my cheery self-reflections: "Deanna, you have a phone call on line one."

I picked up the line. "Hello, hello!"

"Tiana?"

I was only slightly irritated at hearing that name. Sigh. *Sure, okay.* "Yes! It's me." My practiced professionalism kicked in, and I firmly fixed my larger-than-life persona back in place.

"Hello, Tiana. This is Steve's wife."

Steve? Steve was a huge fan who had gone to great lengths to meet me. "Yes, I know Steve, go on." I exclaimed, intent on radiating positive attention for this caller through the phone.

"I thought you should know he killed himself last week."

Her words hung like a damp cloth over the silence of the phone line. I took a deep breath. This was the last thing I expected. "Excuse me?" I replied cautiously.

"Yes, he came home—finally—after I hadn't heard from him in over a week. I had woken up one day, and the entire savings account was drained. The car was gone, and so was my husband. But then he came home in tears, completely remorseful for what he had done—leaving his family to chase a porn star. He said once he met you, he wanted to save you from the sex industry. He assured me that he never cheated on me. He showed me all the autographed porn. He only wanted to make it right. So I asked him to get off all the websites and chat rooms, and that's when he did it. He wasn't able to let go of his porn addiction. Instead he put a gun to his head, said 'I'm sorry,' and shot himself."

He wasn't able to let go of his porn addiction. Instead he put a gun to his head, said 'I'm sorry,' and shot himself.

She fell silent. I had no idea what to say. I couldn't think as my gut clenched tightly in horror and disbelief.

"I am truly sorry, ma'am," was all I could say. I swallowed hard and stayed on the phone as she tried to find as much closure as possible with the situation.

I felt as if I knew Steve fairly well. It was my routine to return home, go to the online chat rooms, and talk with him and a group of fans almost every night. He asked me about my cat, Shirby, and about everything else I loved so dearly. He sent me birthday cards, stuffed animals, and jewelry, but my favorite gifts from fans like him were cat treats. I loved my cat and receiving a gift for her made me feel as if someone knew me—the real me.

I had only been working in the office for a few months when I'd met him in person. The receptionist had told me that he was waiting to meet me at the front of the building. I was thrilled, thrilled to know that somebody thought so highly of me that he'd driven all the way from Georgia to California for the sole purpose of meeting me. I was wearing a sweat suit and had no make-up on. That day, I was focused on working in the office and processing lots of DVD orders. So I gave him a hug and invited him back to watch me work for a day. He had most of my films, and so I autographed every one of them and gave him some posters.

After a few hours, our office manager became a little worried. She said Steve needed to leave. I didn't understand why—but then again, I thought nothing of someone I had never met driving across the country to my place of work to get some signatures. After Steve left, our production assistant continued to keep an eye on me, and he followed me home to make sure no one else was following me.

A couple of days later, a package from Baggin's Gourmet Sandwich Shop arrived for me at the office. Baggin's was a shop halfway between the junior high school and my house. I stopped there some afternoons to grab a twenty-five-cent cookie and a cup of free ice-cold water for the second half of my walk home in the hot Arizona desert. They were my favorite cookies, which Steve had known because I talked about it in the chat rooms. So he went through Tucson on his way back home to Georgia and ordered me a giant box of them. I thought, *He's so sweet! My fans must really love me.*

The problem was, this supposed love wasn't reality. Steve had the unusual experience of transitioning from watching me perform to watching me live my everyday life. And I think that when he told his wife that he wanted to save me, he meant that he'd left my office that day with some fantasy of rescuing me, taking me back to Georgia, and getting me out of the industry for good.

His wife wanted to see his wish fulfilled and offered me a way out. I wasn't sure of her motives: closure, a genuine concern, or honoring her late husband's memory. She said through her tears and grief that maybe I could come to Georgia and marry their son. I laughed as gently as one can in the exchange of processing grief, and I thanked her for the offer. I don't remember how the conversation ended; the whole experience shocked me. After we hung up, I walked down to our office manager to tell her what had happened. When my boss walked in, I told him too. He yelled, "It happens! It's not your fault. Let's get back to sales."

Though my boss's reaction might have seemed insensitive to most (and believe me, it felt insensitive to me at the time, too), I later realized that he hated seeing his loved ones hurt. He became uncomfortable, and when he was uncomfortable, he appeared angry. He had been taught to love in a dysfunctional way, but I understood such dysfunction because I had grown up with it myself. My own dad would rather suck it up and move on and pretend as if all were well instead of talking through a problem, especially if he thought it would bring up pain. His inability to face the truth eventually caused more confusion and pain. Now, here I was with another male authority figure who did the same thing. Talk about repeating dysfunctional patterns. I was drawn to emotionally closed-off male figures.

"Get back to work" is what I certainly did without any further assistance in processing the whole ordeal. I also said farewell to my online chat rooms after this except when I needed to market a new movie I was selling or promote an event where I would appear. Although I was off-camera, I was utilizing my stardom to gain exposure for our company. Steve's wife followed these events and press releases and messaged me every once in a while when she saw me on the cover of a new movie. In the chat rooms, she commented, "I thought Tiana wasn't performing anymore." Sometimes she even called the office. I assured her that the work she saw was either unreleased footage or old footage being reused.

I was still selling sex, not only on screen but in person. I sent girls who told me they had no idea what else to do off to clubs and clients, to fans like this who took their obsessions to new levels. But I was grateful that I no longer had to be physically manhandled. I felt such gratitude for this phase of my life, especially for my new opportunities in business, managing others instead of being managed. I refused to let the words of Steve's wife worry me about the job

I now held—which was, in all reality, simply a new position in a different side of the same broken industry that quite literally discovers people's latest sexual addictions and fetishes and preys on them.

I was so excited to make a name for myself in this business as more than a porn star. I mentally geared up for the task: I knew it would be tough—first, because I was a woman, and second, because I was also in the films myself. A lot of saleswomen who were not in the porn movies themselves traded sex in order to make sales. I refused to do that. I was determined to prove that my DVD sales would be based on trust and hard work. I honestly did want to turn over a new leaf. So I came in early, worked fifty-hour-plus weeks, stayed late, and worked on weekends. I pulled and assessed a lot of reports to learn which states and countries boasted what markets. When necessary, I even helped the warehouse pack orders just to get them out and packaged the way my customers preferred.

Then one day, a man named Dru called me. He wanted to order another set of the show special from the most recent Vegas convention, which was a specially priced offer on one hundred DVDs of our company's choosing. This guy was great at distributing bulk DVD orders, and he did it quickly. But I said the sale was over and apologized just the same, so there was no way I could give him that offer. He laughed. I figured out then that he wouldn't take me seriously, no matter what I said. *Hmmm. I'm not some dumb woman that he can smooth-talk into giving him what he wants*, I thought.

I had regularly encountered plenty of difficult buyers: men who wouldn't take me seriously, who tried to cheat their way out of paying for products, or who tried to trick me with fake invoices. But Dru was a new kind of devious. Rather than taking no for an answer, he fabricated a complaint that he'd never received part of his previous order. I searched the system and found nothing about the supposed missing order that he had described. I quickly told him that we couldn't do anything for him and hung up the phone, proud that I had stood my ground.

But the matter wasn't settled there. In the end, my boss ended up making a deal with Dru over my head—and, to make an embarrassing situation worse, my coworker came in the next day and said he ran into a "Dru from the industry"

125

at a gay bar while he was clubbing. The two gabbed about how difficult I was to work with over Cosmos. Not surprisingly, I lost Dru's business after that. I was furious with my boss and coworker because both had only added more fuel to this customer's sexist fire. When they didn't stand up for me, I learned it might be harder than I thought to be taken seriously in sales.

MY FIRST SALES EXPO

Even so, I wouldn't let them stop me. In September, I was off to my first business trade show. I had explained the problems I'd been having with my boss and male coworkers to my general manager, so I was allowed to go alone. *People will take me seriously now*, I thought. In fact, I was scheduled to meet with about forty customers from around the world and tasked to arrange a deal with them in about twenty minutes, which would result in long-term business for both parties. Not easily done! Many of my competitors made their DVD sales by offering prostitutes to the buyers. Determined to succeed legitimately, however, I tailor-made DVD specials that I knew would sell in their stores, based on what their consumers regularly purchased. I was not interested in a quick order but in a trusting relationship, selling them specifically what would work for them.

> *Many of my competitors made their DVD sales by offering prostitutes to the buyers.*

I arrived at the resort in Scottsdale, Arizona. In no time, people began coming up to me from many companies: DVD chains, mail-order catalogues, and national and international distributors. All of them had the potential to increase my sales (and my income) by hundreds or even thousands a month. And the buyers were so excited to meet me. I had already begun relationship building by being one of the first sales people to call and check in with them each week, so I, too, was excited to meet the people I had been talking with for the past nine months. These representatives had an advantage over me, however—they knew what I looked like from my movies. I had no such advantage to help me identify who was who. As a large group, we headed into the hotel and all converged on the front desk. We picked up our schedules for the week, and then we were off to our suites.

Safely tucked in my room, I kicked off my shoes, got comfortable, and began to focus with great anticipation on the materials I'd been handed. *Oh no.* A sudden surge of dread washed over me as I perused the schedule and the list of companies involved. Dru's company was here. *How nauseating*, I instantly thought. He couldn't cancel our meeting, so I knew for sure that I would spend at least twenty minutes making my wrongs right with him. A grimace stretched unconsciously across my face until I made a quick decision. *Oh well*, I thought, exhaling the breath I had been holding. *Let's have fun for now.* With that, I brushed off my worries and put on my new bikini. I'd packed a different one for each day. After all, it was Arizona, and the resort had a lazy river with my name on it.

Lo and behold, out by the lazy river, I spotted him. Even though we'd never met, I knew I'd identified the right person. That had to be him. My reasoning? He was the best-looking man there.

I assumed he was gay. Surprisingly, he didn't have the Mohawk that my coworker had bragged he was sporting on their night out clubbing. I figured he had just shaved it off, and I admired his choice. I continued to check him out every few minutes and caught him doing the same. In our stubbornness, we avoided each other. I was sure he'd figured out who I was too. In fact, I was right: apparently, I had autographed posters for him and his staff on my first sales visit to his office, so he knew *exactly* who I was. I had been so nervous in my new position as sales manager, I didn't remember meeting him.

Once I left the poolside, nothing improved. Day one was going horribly. People wanted to deal with my boss, not me. I started to cry in one of my meetings, knowing that if I didn't come home with certain results, I'd be fired and have to make movies again. But then I finally got my first order, albeit out of sympathy at my tears. That order gave me confidence and created a ripple effect. Once one order was called in, somehow, more kept coming.

Finally, after a long first day, I was off to celebrate at the bar. I was hanging out with another friend, Chris, who was also a previous performer now-turned-salesman. He seemed to get along great with everyone as he was a lot of fun to be around. My ability to be fun centered on the fact that I had a company credit card and was buying everyone drinks. Eventually, I made my way over to Keith, who was quite influential in the distribution business. He didn't drink, so I offered to buy him a coffee instead.

Keith happened to own the company Dru worked for and, fortunately for me, was super easy to get along with. Even though he was sober, he was also the most entertaining person there. I sipped my cranberry and vodka while he drank his coffee, and we laughed at my newbie stories. In the midst of our enjoyable conversation, in walked Dru, wearing a tight black silk shirt with vertical lines that accentuated his giant upper body. *Man*, I thought, *that is one great-looking guy. Too bad he's gay.* I asked Keith how long Dru had been gay and when he'd gotten rid of his Mohawk. Keith nearly fell on the floor and declared that it was time for me to meet his brother-in-law. He called Dru's cell phone, and we watched him click us to voicemail. We laughed hysterically. When Dru finally caught on, he grudgingly made his way toward us.

Keith repeated my earlier question, and Dru chuckled good-naturedly. Finally, we were all laughing. After nine months of tension with this man, I was amazed that we could enjoy ourselves. Dru was not gay and had never had a Mohawk. My coworker had gone out with somebody else who worked for a different company and just so happened to have the same name. The automatic new release orders that this Dru had canceled after that night were a very strange coincidence.

Dru asked to look at my phone, and I agreed. I also asked if I could buy him a drink, but he did not drink either. So I bought him a Red Bull instead. When I came back, I caught him calling my phone, ready to leave me a voicemail message.

"Did you just steal my phone number?" I asked, slightly incredulous.

I honestly wasn't sure how to feel: imposed on, flattered, taken advantage of, or what. But I had to admit his method to get my phone number was downright hilarious, not to mention slick.

We immediately developed a great friendship and focused all attention on each other as if no one else existed that night. Keith joked about how he'd quickly become a third wheel. He told the other customers that I forgot to ask if he needed anything for the rest of the night. Dru was twenty-four with a few years of sobriety, and his life was "not consumed by" this business, according to him. *Here is a completely normal fellow*, I thought. *But man, it's time for me to go. I have someone else waiting to meet me.* So, professional businesswoman that I was, I slipped away to my next engagement. Now was not the right time to get attached.

CHAPTER FOURTEEN

SOBERING UP

LATER THAT NIGHT, Anthony was waiting for me back at the hotel room. He was the first guy I'd dated since I had sworn off all relationships years ago when I first became a serious performer. At least, I thought we were dating. Up to this point, we had created a routine: I would fly or take a train from Los Angeles to San Diego every other weekend to see him. He talked to me about interesting things, like my spirituality and my smaller-than-mustard-seed-sized faith. Of course, after we'd both had a few drinks, all spirituality went out the window. I was at his beck and call in the hopes that this could turn into a serious relationship. I didn't want any more one-night stands. As a requested buyer, he had been invited to this business expo too. This show was not the relationship debut I had hoped for. He claimed it would be unprofessional to be seen together in public. And because I was used to secret relationships, I didn't question him.

Whenever Anthony and I met up at the expo, he told me about the other hot salesgirls. He asked if they could join us after he'd gone off with them while expecting me to wait for him back at our room. He was disappointed when I said no. I went to the strip club with him and the other buyers the next night, hoping to win his attention back, but he only degraded me later for talking to him too much in public and for getting drunk and jealous. Terrified that

I would lose both him and my job, I begged my new friend Chris for some cigarettes to help me calm down. I smoked until I sobered up while Chris gave me inside tips for my first trade show.

Meanwhile, Dru had taken to texting me a daily play-by-play of his experiences at the expo. His on-going commentary cracked me up. But I told myself I couldn't respond much, because I didn't want to be disrespectful to the guy I was trying to date. So I laughed off his stories and kept our relationship as professional as possible. He made it really tough, though. He met me before each meal and walked me to the dinners. Then he texted me from the table next to mine and asked how my sales meetings were going. I told him they would be better if I got off my phone. We shot a quick glance at each other, smiled, and went about our business.

Eventually, I had worked through my schedule right up to the time of my official meeting with Dru. We were both in bad shape: I was hung over, and he was tired from being up all night, paranoid that the stripper he took home from the club was going to steal his wallet and Rolex. I was so jaded by this industry that I did not once think this was a red flag for a man I was growing fond of. Then again, I was autographing naked pictures of myself for the buyer's stores, so who was I to judge? We conducted some company business during our scheduled twenty-minute meeting. He put me back on his regular shipment list—the very same one I thought he had purposefully removed me from. Once we finished business, we made a plan to go swimming together later.

I showed up at his hotel room at 4:00 p.m. and waited outside for him to get some towels for us. He invited me in, but I knew better. I didn't want people to think that we were a couple or that I was available to go inside another man's hotel room. I only wanted to be his friend. He grabbed some towels and did a few push-ups, and we were on our way. He grabbed my arm and skipped—yes, skipped!—with me all the way to the pool. He was a six-foot-two, 225-pound man skipping. How could I not let my guard down after that?

After our swim, we separated for a bit and met up later at the group dinner. My shoe heel had broken off on my walk over, so he left the dinner and walked two miles with me to buy some Super Glue. I bought him a pack of cigarettes to repay him for his kindness and decided it was officially time for me to pick up smoking again too.

MY LAST DRINK

Now that we were both smokers, we also agreed we would quit when we returned home. Even better, we would make sure to hold each other accountable. After the show ended, we both quickly returned to our normal routines in the hustle and bustle of Los Angeles. Shipping and selling, selling and shipping. And yet all the while, he was still texting me play-by-play accounts of his day. He went on dates and texted me private commentary such as, "My date's hand is sweaty." I told him that it was probably because she was angry he was on his phone.

"Stop it!" I'd half-tease, while fully enjoying myself. Though we stayed in almost constant contact, he lived his life, and I lived mine.

September 30, 2006, just a few short weeks after returning from Arizona, the mother of all parties was happening, and *I* had been invited. A legendary rock star teamed up with a porn company to hold a release party at his house. I went with a magazine editor I'd previously dated in the beginning of my career, knowing full well that this would be the night I'd lose the no-smoking bet I'd made with Dru. I lit up, put on a short skirt and a shirt with no bra, and I was on my way. When I arrived, there was Anthony, the guy I was dating. He had told me that I couldn't come down to San Diego that weekend but failed to explain why. I now knew the reason: He had flown to town for this party without even telling me. I couldn't believe that after all the money I'd spent going to see him, he had just shown up at a party in Los Angeles, hoping I wouldn't be there. I was infuriated.

He went off in the corner, doing lines of coke with porn stars, and I wasn't sure if I was more shocked or angry. He knew my history with drugs. And he knew how I felt about him. *Ughhh!* I fled the scene, deciding to have fun without him and without the drugs. The host had hired all kinds of servers and performers for the party, including men on stilts and Cirque de Soleil entertainers. They were serving a pink tequila that was debuting at the party, and since alcohol was another matter altogether for me, I grabbed as many shots as I could. Then

I drank the cups of alcohol people left on the stage, even those with cigarettes in them. Soon, the musicians were performing their hit songs, and I started dancing on poles in front of a ton of my buyers—the very same buyers I was trying to make an impression on and present myself to as a professional.

The next thing I knew, I went from spinning on a pole to sprawled out on the floor in another room. Within minutes—or was it hours?—I had passed out, puked all over this famous guy's floor, and was being tended to by a crew of people. They kept asking me if I'd done any drugs. Another porn star took advantage of my drama. *"I didn't overdose this time!"* she proudly announced in the background.

> *I looked at the IVs in my arm, the machines attached to my heart, and then their faces —and I cried.*

I started yelling, "I don't do drugs! I don't do drugs!" But then the sirens grew louder as the ambulance pulled up. *Oh, crap.* Reporters were everywhere. *Please, please don't let them see me.* The magazine editor I came with and some other friends kindly put a sheet over my face so that no one could see who was being rushed to the emergency room.

I woke up to the faces of the kind actor I'd last performed with and his wife. I looked at the IVs in my arm, the machines attached to my heart, and then their faces— and I cried. "I don't want to live anymore. I am so tired of being here. *Please,* God, just take me!" I sobbed, in distressed delirium. Then I felt myself drifting off. I'd asked God to take me, and I truly thought he'd answered my prayer.

But instead, God had a different plan. The next day, I woke up, filled with remorse and in a ton of pain. I was not sure how I had gotten home from the hospital. When Anthony called that morning to harass me, I told him I was done. Then Dru called to check on me, and I told him what a jerk Anthony was. He said, "Don't worry about him. Let's worry about you."

By now, Dru had about five years of sobriety under his belt. When we first talked at the show during the conference, Dru had said, "I don't understand how you call yourself clean from drugs, but you still drink."

I'd responded, "Well, I don't have a problem with *alcohol*. I have a drug problem." But of course, I was wrong. On the phone now, Dru asked me if he could take me to get some help. "I don't need help with my alcohol," I confidently said, sensing that a real change had occurred deep within me. But I sensed something else, too—a yearning springing up. My voice softened and true vulnerability spilled out in my next words. "But could you please take me to church?"

I had checked out a church earlier that year when a former performer and neighbor of mine left the business to connect with God. I called her the day I decided to quit filming because my godmother had suggested that I go to church. My initial response to my godmother was, "I can't go to church and work in this business!"

In response, she sent me a copy of *The Purpose Driven Life* and told me, "Deanna, if we weren't sick, we wouldn't need church. That's where you go to *get* well, not where you go when you are already well." So I called up my friend, and I went.

After the first time I had attended a service, I signed up for a women's retreat and even joined a life group, trying to move forward. Everyone wanted me out of the business, but no one actually walked me through the process of what that would look like. I went to church on Sunday and then turned around and took topless photos with rock stars at golf tournaments the next day. At the next life group, I told them how a famous drummer, a fan of Tiana's, called me at work and asked me out. "Don't worry, though. I told him I wasn't free. I had plans with the pastor and his wife, so I threw away his number," I said triumphantly.

Since they were big fans, they laughed and said, "Next time, invite him to group."

What I did with that number was definitely for the best. I was fighting a huge battle with addiction to attention and fame. My response was as instant as a newly sober addict who comes across drugs and immediately flushes them down the toilet. I had a record of being a very outrageous groupie, so I knew that it was a bad idea to go out with him. Still, in the next minute, I thought, *Maybe I could talk to him about God.* Then just as quickly, *No, no . . . no missionary dating—focus on your own relationship with God, Deanna.* As I participated in life group, I began to absorb some truths about God. I shared what I'd learned at church over the weekend with my coworkers as well as with all my buyers. They kindly listened and shared their own insights.

Without knowing how to live a godly lifestyle outside church, my attendance became sporadic and half-hearted. But now, in the moment Dru offered help to me, I realized I was ready to try church again. Dru agreed both to take me to church and to show me what fun without alcohol could look like. He also reminded me that I had officially lost the smoking bet and that I owed him fifty dollars. "How about dinner instead?" I suggested. He somehow talked me into five dinners and paying him ten dollars cash on top of that. I was thrilled to have five guaranteed nights with him—and unlike Anthony, he was local, so who knew what would happen? Maybe it would lead to more.

He brought some tennis rackets and a pack of smokes over to my apartment since I had lost our bet and it was over. We "played tennis," but I basically chased a lot of balls. He was so athletic. On the other hand, I was uncoordinated with a lot of energy to burn. When we were done, we ran upstairs to my apartment to get ready for church. On our way up the stairs, he tripped and fell down. *Smack!* I couldn't help but laugh. This was the smoothest man I knew, and he'd tripped. *He is so adorable!* I thought, as though it were the most natural reaction in the world. It was the first—but not the last—time he made a fool of himself around me. All his moves in our relationship seemed to have been inspired by Will Smith's character in *Hitch,* the one who went from cool and calm, leader of love, to disastrous on his own dates.

MY ORIGINAL ADDICTION

My desire for church went away when I saw how uninterested *he* was after attending two services. I wanted a life that included God, but I didn't want to do it alone. I also loved how I felt when I spent time with someone and could be myself. I was discovering myself as a girl and not as a porn performer, and he seemed to be all the help I needed. I was laughing at the simple things of life, and everything became smooth and easy, for the moment at least. When the pain subsided, so did my motivation to embark on a new way of living. With Dru, I felt normal and accepted as if I had nothing to prove or to change about myself.

After a month of our friendship, I went on one of many adult-video-chain tours out of state. I met different buyers, checked out their stores, and maximized profit on my former character by autographing movies during the evening hours. Dru kept in touch the whole time I was gone. He made sure that I was sober and okay each evening. When the weekend ended, his true colors started to show. Since I was in stardom mode, he figured that he would ask me if I could get him into the Playboy mansion. My stomach dropped. *He really doesn't like me. He likes the actress.* I intentionally ignored his comment and brought his attention back to me.

After three more weeks of chatting and goofing around, I talked Dru into taking a day off to go with me and another friend to Disneyland. I thought it would be appropriate since a big part of our friendship was discovering activities outside of porn. He had just told me a bedtime story the other night on the phone, and the story ended with the princess (me) swept off her feet by a handsome prince (him) who was wandering around the park. His brother-in-law and sister (his bosses) were thrilled he was going to take a day off. He never did that, and he needed a break.

He picked me up as usual in his Mercedes SL350, top down and with Akon blaring. We ran around both amusement parks and played every game. I loved every minute of it, since carnival games are my favorite thing in the world to do. We jumped in the giant letters that spelled C-A-L-I-F-O-R-N-I-A and went on kids' rides. Then, after a rousing game of hand-smacking and goofing off, we boarded the Ferris wheel. Too late, I learned that the seats on this particular Ferris wheel flipped over. I ran to his side of the cart, and he held me and rested his head on top of mine. It was our first moment of chemistry, and with it, came the decision that it was time for me to let go of reservations and give in to what was so obviously happening between us.

This was the right day to make it official. I showed him I was interested in the only way I knew how. I tried to seduce him and reverted to my old teasing behaviors. Inside, I was horrified at myself, which he would throw in my face for the rest of our relationship. But I was so confused at that stage of life that I didn't know any better. Luckily, we didn't do much more than kiss. I managed to cut it short, and then I left him at the front step of my apartment and closed the door before I could go any further. After that night, I considered us an official couple.

On our fourth official date, I showed him my STD test. He was totally flabbergasted. "What is this?" was all he managed to get out.

"I'm ready to move to the next level, and I need you to know that I am clear," I said, as the waiter at Black Angus cleared the appetizer plates to make room for our main dish. Dru was shocked that I would carry the test around with me, but it was normal for porn performers. In any case, after a few questions about my health history and the Hep C scare, Dru and I skipped the movie we planned on seeing after dinner and went straight to my place.

I know that it was because something deep inside my soul said, "Don't do this. It will only hurt." I also know it wasn't something but Someone—God.

As we started to heat up, I realized this wasn't a movie scene for me. This was real life, and I was developing genuine feelings for this man. I didn't want to go through with this after all. I covered my face with my hands, panicking. He stopped when he noticed, and I felt horrible. I was doing it again. *Why do I offer myself to men and then back down?*

In retrospect, I know that it was because something deep inside my soul said, "Don't do this. It will only hurt." I also know it wasn't *something* but *Someone*— God. The God who I had prayed to whenever I faced the harshest realities of my life. He was trying to warn me—not out of anger, but out of love—because he knew the damage it would cause my heart. But I shoved the feelings and the tender warning away, burying them in a deep corner of myself, before assuring

Dru that it was only a moment of nervousness. We proceeded as planned. After we were done, he got dressed and ready to leave.

"What? You're just going to leave me now?" I said, hardly able to keep the shock and desperation from my voice. "You have got to be kidding. Please, please don't do this to me. You don't understand what it will do," I begged. I was desperate for him to stay, knowing that the moment he left, our relationship wouldn't be the same. *I* wouldn't be the same.

He insisted he had to leave, but he promised to return and stay the coming weekend. This pattern continued for the first few months of our relationship. He came over, stayed about an hour with me or sometimes the whole night, and left early in the morning. He never invited me to his place. He came up with reasons why I couldn't come over, such as his roommate had left the place a mess. Though I knew he had a female roommate, I didn't question him about it. I wasn't ready to face the truth I knew deep within. Instead I took the passive-aggressive route—wearing as much glitter as possible on nights I knew he would pick me up so that anyone who got into his Mercedes or who saw him the next day would see that I had been there.

He continued to show me how to have fun apart from porn and alcohol, such as going to pumpkin patches and pretending to be lost around the city. Neither of us could admit we didn't want the night to end. In turn, I showed him what I thought was the glamorous side of the industry by getting him into VIP parties and clubs in Hollywood. We went to most of these parties together and ordered non-alcoholic beverages. I took pictures, walked the red carpet, did interviews, and wore flashy clothes.

Seven months into our relationship, I finally found out the truth, or at least part of what Dru had kept hidden. So many lies were involved that I don't know if I will ever learn the full story. One day, my sales partner asked me if I knew Dru was married. Wasting no time, I messaged him. He didn't respond; instead his boss called my general manager to find out what was going on. He asked why Dru's personal life was coming up at work, a life my coworkers and his knew about, but I didn't. After hearing about this conversation, I went into my GM's office, crying and asking how long they had known.

Everyone in the company knew that he was in a long-term relationship, but no one had the heart to tell me. With this much of the truth finally out in the open, my dad and my new step-mom suggested that I do a background check on him. I didn't find much, but I did discover another name on his house. I eventually got him on the phone and asked him to explain himself.

He admitted that yes, he was in a committed relationship and had been for five years. They shared a house and bank accounts. Then he justified his behavior and said, "Well, I never said we were exclusive." But that was not my understanding at all. Shocked, I needed time to pull myself together. I had permission to take the rest of the day off, and when I reached my apartment, I called him back, only to get his voicemail. I broke it off, swearing that I would absolutely not be in a relationship with him as long as he was dating her. As I was breaking up with him, I finally admitted for the first time that I loved him and that this was breaking my heart. He left me a message a few minutes later with the same sentiments. He didn't want our relationship to end, but he refused to ask me to stay. The exchange left me angry at the world. *Are you kidding? This is the end? This is love?* I didn't understand what was happening—what *was* this crazy, emotional, love-filled disaster?

It was merely the first of many cycles of break-ups and reunifications between us. We'd fight, break up, and then run into each other months later at a DVD trade show. I once brought a peace offering, a gift for him, when I knew he'd be at a show: a money clip from Ben Bridges. He'd bought my first Christmas gift there, a gift he told me not to tell anyone about. It had been my first real ring, zipped inside a teddy bear. Even though we weren't together anymore, I wanted to give him something to remember me by—something manly and classy. The money clip had a beautiful diamond and an inscription on the back, *May you always prosper*. He worked hard for money, and it was important to him. He expressed love to others by giving lavish gifts and money, so I thought it wasn't right for him to carry his wad of one hundred dollar bills in a rubber band. The gift was sensible and would ensure he thought of me often throughout the day. Sure enough, his attention was now back on me.

I learned that no matter how much time passed between break ups, when we saw each other, it was as if no one else existed all over again. I didn't need gifts; his presence was enough. We'd begin a friendly game of chase and act like kids, running around convention halls and city streets and through water fountains. By each show's end, we'd be back together again.

BACK TO DEANNA

It had been four months since our latest break up when he finally made the decision to officially break off his relationship with the other woman. We began to spend time together during the week at his place. We decorated it and started to build a home. Then we had what I call "The Fight"—the fight that would be a continual theme for the rest of our relationship. We ran into someone I knew at BJ's, and as soon as the guy headed back to his table, Dru asked resentfully, "Is that someone you had sex with in a movie?" The coldness of his comment sparked a burning fury in my veins.

I retaliated by slinging his early deception about his ex back at him. *How dare he throw my past in my face?* The dinner was over.

After I finished crying to my parents on the phone while curled up in a corner on his bathroom floor, we agreed to have an honest conversation and address the root of these issues. He admitted that he'd been uncomfortable at all the parties we'd gone to as he felt like I was trying to get everyone's attention but his. I told him that was simply not the case. I desperately wanted him to be proud of me, the girl he was with. I thought if everyone else told him how lucky he was, he might want to keep me. At this point, I realized I wanted to be done going to these events, to stop autographing, to start using my real name only, and to finally settle down.

We were in agreement. I threw out my seven-inch heels and porn wear. He took me to Ann Taylor and bought me respectable clothes. I felt so honored, knowing that he wanted me all to himself. I finally dropped the name Tiana for good. It was Deanna's time to shine.

He slowly tried to tear me away from my past. He could not handle knowing about it, seeing it at work, and hearing about it from others. He was tormented by my shame. And to be honest, so was I.

We were ready to begin house hunting so that we could move in together. We thought that just maybe, if I moved out of the valley and if he moved out of the house he had shared with his ex, we could move into the future we were fighting so hard for.

CHAPTER FIFTEEN

THE NEXT STEP

"**D**RU! WHERE ARE YOU?" I shouted in exasperation as I came walking into the new house he had bought for us, only to find he was not home once again. Frustrated and confused, I called my friend to help me make sense of what was going on.

"Tracy, you don't understand," I complained, drawing out the last word for emphasis. "He's not the same person anymore. I moved in, and he doesn't call or text me anymore. He's barely ever here. It's like I never even knew him! He seems like a stranger." She had no answers for me. But someone else did.

Dru's sister came over and invited me to a family meeting at her house down the street. When I expressed thoughts similar to those I'd shared with Tracy, she said, "You're right, Deanna. He is not the same—and with good reason."

Oh yeah? You mean I'm not imagining things? Finally, we're getting somewhere! I thought, eager to understand.

"He's been drinking," she said simply. As her words registered, my whole world tilted off-kilter.

"He got addicted to pain medication this year, and in an effort to come off it, he began drinking," she tried to explain.

143

Noooo! I screamed inside. I bit my lip and tried to blink back the tears threatening to pool in my eyes. *No! Not* that *answer*, my heart cried.

I couldn't believe it. This was the same guy who'd helped me stay sober at every party. *How could this be true?* I wondered, even as I saw the answer loud and clear on his sister's face. It was an ugly, painful irony: I had almost a year-and-a-half of sobriety under my belt, and he'd been using the whole time. How much more of our relationship was a lie? As the lies and the truth emerged into the light, they both made me ache inside.

But the signs were all around me. I found Nyquil bottles everywhere: in kitchen cabinets, strewn on my bathroom counter, and in his car. As fast as I threw them out, they always reappeared. He also threw up constantly after he ate—so much so, that I thought he was bulimic. Now I realized it was from all the Vicodin he was taking. I didn't think anything of it at the time, but now I remembered the night two months into our relationship when we were at our first AVN show together. He got some pills from one of his supposedly sober friends, and after taking them, he said, "This is the best I have felt in a long time."

That night, I'd thought, *Won't this lead to relapse?* But who was I to say anything? I'd only been sober for a couple months at the time, and he had been for years!

Now, I panicked. I didn't know who I was more worried about—him or me. The great mental obsession of an alcoholic's mind was back in my life, staring me down, as it emerged from the sinister shadows I'd fought to keep at bay. Only, I didn't *want* to drink again. I really didn't. The old me thought, *What happened to the ride-or-die girl I was when I was a teenager? The one who wouldn't let her man go out on his own?* But I eschewed those thoughts firmly. No, the old me was gone: I resolved that I *would not* drink. So what was the next plan?

The family meeting where I learned the truth was the first of many such gatherings as we tried to figure out how to help him. Some family members asked me not to leave him, because it would be detrimental to his health. Yet I was the one who had to lie awake in our bed for months while he snuck out and left me at home. This caused one anxiety attack after another for me as I worried that another loved one would end up dead.

Dru's closest family members with thirteen-plus years of sobriety also relapsed as did others at their company. They had all supported each other in their sobriety journey. Once one of them fell, so did all the rest. I didn't understand what was happening. They were all trying to hide it, but everyone was distancing themselves from me. I was fighting for my life, trying to keep from sliding back, too, all while living in this giant, empty house that would never become the home I had hoped for. As his sister confessed what caused her relapse, she brought me to some local recovery meetings. She knew if I didn't get help, I would definitely be next.

At times, I felt close to going insane and almost went to the hospital. Dru would come home with his lies, ready to fight off any argument I had prepared, and I'd leave, both of us in tears. We fought constantly, and I ran away and moved out (temporarily) at least once a month whenever the stress became too great. Finally, I became so fed up with the cycle that I left for what I intended to be the last time. Then I continued seeking support from the group his sister introduced me to in order to stay away from a drink and to battle the suicidal thoughts that attacked me. I constantly felt as if I were on the brink of insanity—so much so, that some days, running in front of a bus actually seemed like a viable option.

He had been molested himself as a young boy, so he thought recreating these scenarios was indulging some high-demand fantasies of a certain population.

Everyone else around me was relapsing; people at my work were going to rehab. My boss was beginning to feel deep sorrow for the movies he was shooting that portrayed girls as young as his daughter. He had been molested himself as a young boy, so he thought recreating these scenarios was indulging some high-demand fantasies of a certain population. He sat with tears in his eyes as he told me his sad story and then pulled out a bottle of pills he took to mask his feelings. This began a long series of brain scans, rehabs, and doctors to help him find what was wrong with him—to help him find a reason

145

why he never had peace or relief, even though he had fame and money.

By 2008, while everyone was crumbling around me, I went back to church. I only went for a few weeks whenever hard times hit, but their doors and hearts were always open to me. I joined a purity group. I thought if I stayed accountable with both sexual relationships and with substance use, I could keep moving forward and not be pulled back into more self-induced pain. I genuinely found I no longer wanted to be distracted by men.

All this led me to the realization that it was time to think about other career options besides the porn industry. I wasn't ready yet to fully leave—but I began to think about it and to take small steps away from it. I started taking classes at a local community college. I was earning certifications in one area after another, working my way toward a degree in health. I also picked up the copy of the book my godmother had given me earlier, *The Purpose Driven Life* by Rick Warren. It was time to make sense of my life again.

I read about baptism: the importance of dying to the old life so that in Christ, I could rise to new life. I was in, ready to make that commitment in front of the entire church. The pastor asked why I was making this decision, and through my pain-filled tears, I was barely able to utter, "I am so tired of doing it my way." I was submerged in the water. I felt as if everything would be okay and that I no longer had to fight. Jesus would do that for me. I had a part, too, but I had no idea what that looked like. Despite my beginning attempts at surrender, I still had a long way to go. The battle continued.

Even after my baptism, I went back to work as usual. Only now, my heart was starting to break for what I was seeing and hearing each day: directors talking about the violent things they could do, such as stepping on a girl's neck, to get reactions. Though it was illegal to sell the kind of footage they were discussing in the U.S., it was not illegal in Europe. In this way, they could portray the sounds and expressions that would feed the demands in the U.S. of those who wanted to take the demeaning of women to the next twisted level.

I could no longer watch the movies I was selling, but I still didn't feel done yet. Maybe I was here to tell others about God. Maybe I was the light in a dark place. I told my coworkers and even my distributors about my decision, and they were happy for me. But then it was back to business for us and time for the next AVN convention, which meant that it was also time to face Dru again. It had been three months since we'd officially ended our relationship—the longest we had gone without speaking in the eighteen months we had known each other.

CULMINATING PAIN

By this time, I had a sponsor in recovery, who told me to check in with her each night I was in Vegas for the conference. I did just that. I didn't have to hide what I was doing when I talked with her. She knew that if I continued to be honest, stay sober, and seek an authentic relationship with God, he would reveal the rest. Temptation was all around me, but support was only a phone call away. Praise God. I could not have done it alone, and I didn't have to.

At the conference, Dru spent the majority of the time partying, while I cried in every meeting from the pain of seeing his destruction. Many people had known about our relationship, so several asked me about it. When they did, I broke down. If they were close to either of us, the second the door shut and provided some privacy for the conversation, rivers flowed from my eyes. I became utterly helpless over the pain of losing him and couldn't do my job. By the time the show ended, I was exhausted from the emotional stress. Thankfully, I had already scheduled time after my return, self-aware enough to recognize that with the routine mental breakdowns I was having, I would need it.

While still at the conference, I had also felt I needed to make amends with Dru's best friend, Chris. Making amends was an important part of recovery. Chris then helped me get through the rest of the weekend. He was the same friend who had shown me the ropes of the distribution business when we were in Arizona at my first business expo. He also became friends with Dru at that time, but their friendship later enabled destructive drinking habits for both of them. It had been so easy to blame Chris for Dru's addiction, yet I knew it wasn't his fault. I apologized for all the times I had gotten mad and blamed him for Dru's stupid drunk escapades and foolish decisions. Chris apologized for keeping him out all hours of the night and for the pain of our breakup. He said he was going through similar relationship troubles.

His phone rang, and he got in a fight with his girlfriend right in front of me. She ended the call with, "I hope you die." I tried to comfort him by sharing how I was coping with the emotions of my too-public breakup in the industry. Words were all I had to offer.

I left the trade show and returned to gambling in the casino below my hotel room. But a short time later, Chris somehow managed to get my number and call me. In my emotional state of mind, I was happy to have a friend contact me—especially one who was in as much pain as I was and who could understand what I was going through. We flew home together and naturally began to re-evaluate our lives to see what was next.

He quit his job with one of the top porn companies in the business, deciding the pay wasn't worth the stress. He rested at my house for a few days until he felt like taking his next step. He was the first guy I'd talked to in a few months since my break up with Dru, so when he came to stay, I completely fell apart and pushed myself on him. For a few moments, sex allowed me to escape my pain, only to cry hysterically that I wasn't ready to be with anyone else. Instead I was causing myself more pain, and once I realized this, I stopped. He didn't push for more and stayed to hang out with me anyway.

CRAWLING BACK

A loud and abrupt knock at the door startled me late one night. Chris was already asleep. Who could this be?

I opened the door, confused and cautious because of the hour. It was Dru. *How did he get in?* I wondered, since I lived in a gated community. I learned quickly that he and his friend were looking for Chris since his phone had been off and no one had heard from him since he quit his job. Dru speared me with a hateful look when he spotted Chris passed out on the couch, and the venom in his eyes screamed, "I always knew you were a whore." My insides shuddered under his gaze while his unspoken message registered deep in my core.

At that moment, I felt as if I *was* exactly what he believed of me. He was right.

I was worthless. Though I didn't drown my sorrows in a drink, I did indulge my pain by finishing my affair with Chris. It was no use pretending to be someone I was not.

I continued this relationship with Chris for two months until I couldn't do it anymore. The affair was no longer numbing my pain, and even though we had begun to care for each other, it didn't seem as if either of us was going to settle down anytime soon. Instead, I was making increasingly poor decisions in an attempt to escape. Almost anything was becoming permissible with me or around me. It would only be a matter of time before I added more affairs to the equation, and then eventually, I would return to filming movies to try to escape again. I could sense the danger ahead like a dark, swirling cloud, ready to devour all the light. I was turning back into the old me. I had to walk away from Chris.

I longed to return to being the girl I had been with Dru before everything had fallen apart—a normal girlfriend. With him, I didn't resort to being a porn star because he didn't like it. Sure, the relationship was hostile at times, but I wanted to focus on the positive aspects of our relationship.

Even so, in many ways, our relationship was similar to my other relationships. I was still trying to live a normal life in a dysfunctional industry. At the core, we were two unhealthy people, trying to hold onto the only version of love we knew.

When I had lived with him, we fought about his drug use. He had called me vulgar names in front of his friends, and the second I got angry and threatened to leave, he threw my things on the roof so I couldn't. Other times, he hovered over me, got very close to my face, and yelled in an effort to intimidate me. I once kicked him in the knees in fear, then ran and hid, trembling in the closet. Other nights, he locked himself in the bedroom, and I would pound on the door for hours. I'd threaten to leave, and he'd act like he was going to run me over with his car. I often called the cops before the situation got too out of control. By that point, I had come to know that angry, glazed-over look in his eyes. I broke things around the house, and he flicked lit cigarettes at my face. He knew I loved my animals more than anything, so he tossed my cats out the door to scare them because he knew it would hurt me. This dysfunctional cycle repeated for another three years.

However, I told myself the pain of trying to do life without him was worse than the pain of being together. At least I wasn't a whore when I was with Dru. I was faithful, trying to be the best person I could be. We *needed* each other. Both of us fell to our lowest levels since our breakup, acting out in our pain. I wanted to pursue my original goals of creating a healthy life and challenge him to do the same. I began attending support groups for those in relationships with active addicts. I wasn't going to try to change him; I was going to love him through it. I moved back in with Dru by that fall, only ten months after my baptism.

The proposal came a few weeks later. He was acting sketchy as usual, and so was his cousin, who was also living with us. He typically went off to do drugs with this guy. In fact, he had recently come home with cocaine—but after that, he had said he would get clean for a while. This particular night, I figured they were high again. I was furious, but he suggested we go out, and I resentfully agreed. We went to our favorite Mexican restaurant where a wedding reception happened to be taking place. Dru made some smug comment about "the poor loser," referring to the groom and the idea of marriage. He'd made a similar negative comment about marriage just a few days earlier. *Why am I sticking around if he really doesn't think there's a future for us?* Little did I know that he was trying to throw me off track for what he had planned.

Since we couldn't eat at the Mexican restaurant (our first choice), we opted instead for an expensive Italian restaurant that I had always wanted to try. But once we arrived, my anger killed my appetite, so we walked it off in the beautifully lit town of Valencia instead.

Every few feet, he'd stop to comment about how many people were around. I thought he was either being paranoid or that something big was about to happen. Then he did it. He pulled out the ring while we were standing in front of the chocolate shop, staring at all the delicious-looking morsels behind the glass. I shrieked, "What? What is *that*?" I put my anger on the back burner at the surprise and gladly accepted, assuring him that I would be by his side forever. We'd made it through this much, nearly three years of ups and downs.

It could only get better from here, right? He called my parents to tell them the news and to assure them that they didn't have to worry—he would take care of me financially for the rest of my life. He thought that as long as I had the roof of a giant house over my head, all the fine dining I wanted, and money at my disposal, I would have everything I needed.

Only life kept getting worse for another whole year. He was addicted to drugs, and I was addicted to him. He continued to degrade me when he was insecure, making such comments as, "Why don't you go call your pimp?" The lies continued each week and so did the detoxing and venting his anger on me. I began to hate sex more and more because he asked me to do things that he claimed I "had no problem doing in the movies." I was in physical and emotional pain, with no idea if I had just been with him or with the drugs he was on. My cooperation assured him that I wanted him more than the guys in the movies, at least temporarily. He justified his treatment of me by making statements like, "At least I'm not hitting you," or "I treat you better than any other boyfriend ever did. At least I can provide anything you will ever need."

He was addicted to drugs, and I was addicted to him.

If I thought of running again, he reminded me of my deepest insecurities. "No one will ever love you, because they will never get over your past." He definitely hurt me more than any customer ever had by how he spoke to me and treated me like a prostitute. Enraged, I'd throw my engagement ring at him. He retaliated by breaking my phone. I didn't need to move out anymore because now I had another playing card: breaking off the engagement and living upstairs in our huge house until he apologized or until I caved. This was our new cycle.

In desperate attempts to learn a healthy way to love each other and to heal from the damage we continued to bring to the relationship, we sought out one counselor after another. We could not figure out why our relationship wasn't working. He went in and out of detox, and I worked hard to keep myself out of a mental institution. I'd argue with Dru about his drug addiction, and he would throw my legitimate prescription drug use for anti-depressants and anti-anxiety drugs back in my face. When I started attending support groups, I had made a decision to use a holistic approach to improving my mental health and to stop taking all prescriptions for depression, psychotic episodes, insomnia, and anxiety. Recovery had given me a way of living in the worst of situations without resorting to any type of chemical dependency, no matter how legitimate. I'd actually learned how to cope with the attacks until I could grasp what was causing them, and I worked hard to continue improving my new skills.

Somehow, every effort we made led to more fights. But after every fight, we'd try again. We'd return to work and try to maintain a professional relationship there. Then we would come home and sleep in separate rooms.

In January 2010, we attended another Vegas show. While there, we clearly saw that it was time for me to completely leave the business. I was tired of dodging fans with cameras and of dealing with directors and company owners who thought they could grab me whenever and however forcefully they wanted. A business suit alone wouldn't earn me the respect I wanted in this industry. A producer grabbed me by the hair in front of all my buyers. That was the last straw for both Dru and me. Despite feedback from male and female performers, directors, and producers that I'd never find a job outside this business, I had been training for a couple years under our company's personal trainer. I was honing my skills in the health industry and felt ready to put those certifications and experience to use. I also had four years of hard work and solid sales management skills under my belt. If work in the health and fitness industry didn't pan out, I could find a sales job outside the industry using my administrative and people skills.

LIFE OUTSIDE THE SEX INDUSTRY

Keeping it quiet until last minute, I left the sex industry in March 2010 and became a homemaker: the job I had always wanted. I joined a new church closer to where we lived, and I got plugged in for real this time. I was living the Stepford dream and was finding ways to make the most of my life. I helped others in my support groups heal and recover from alcohol, and a few of these women were even baptized. They, in turn, led others to baptism. I joined Bible studies on how to be a better wife (even though I wasn't one) and brought Dru with me to the relationship series as well as to other classes offered through the church that I thought would benefit us.

I began to pray for Dru's brother-in-law and sister as they were discovering life outside the shadiness of the porn world. They had spent decades in the industry and struggled to tell who their friends were and who only wanted something from them. I prayed for them to experience peace, joy, and a drama-free life—true happiness with fellow peers. I prayed for them to find friends who would love them for who they were, friends they could trust and let in. These types of genuine, selfless friendships were hard to find in that line of work.

They got back into recovery themselves. They adopted a baby, and then two churches launched right in their new neighborhood, one of them through my church. I lit up inside. Those days of praying face down on the cold bathroom tile floor were proving fruitful. I was beyond thrilled that they were going to see how deep and wide and great God's love was for them. Dru saw my excitement and joined me as much as he could with the church plant. He honestly wanted a better future for us, but he could not break free from the pain pills. As his fiancée, I kept looking for ways to make him happy, but I cringed and jumped in fear anytime he came near me affectionately. My nightmares were off the charts, and I was suffering from night terrors. I thought I was ruined forever. Dru was always telling me what a terrible person I was and how hard it was to be with me. My PTSD convinced me he was right. I was not lovable. No one would want to live with me.

My health and fitness business was now ready to launch, so I put all my focus there. At least in this area, life was looking up, and my client list was growing. The gym Dru and his dad had built for me in our house was officially making money. I was now attending church, neighborhood, and work events that had nothing to do with porn. But Dru was still in the business and on pills, so we grew further and further apart. He had no desire anymore to engage in life while, at the same time, I was gaining a sense of what it was like to be part of something and contribute to society. I was tired of hiding, living in fear that someone would find out who I used to be. I was diving all the way in.

Any time I gained confidence in my new life outside of porn, Dru told me all men looked at me like a sex object. I was beginning to realize that he was projecting his attitude toward women on me. He was so jaded by porn that he viewed all women this way. I might put on a nice dress simply because I loved to dress up. But instead of complimenting me, he asked, "Who are you trying to impress?" If I sported my new limited edition Juicy Couture sweat suit around town, he told me exactly what men would think the second I left the house. I couldn't win. I couldn't get him to see me for who I was. He didn't look at me the way he had when we first met. People at the grocery store were more excited to talk to me than he was.

We had nothing in common anymore except our toxic infatuation with each other. When so much was finally right in my world, I couldn't bring myself to see that he was the one thing still so totally wrong.

CHAPTER SIXTEEN

ENDING THE CYCLE

"**D**EAR LORD, PLEASE, *please*, just make this clear to me. Tell me what I need to do to make this relationship right!" Now I was even begging. At the beginning of that scorching summer in 2011, I was praying out loud in my car as I sat in the parking lot of Real Life Church, waiting to meet with the family care pastor. Dru and I had given everything we could to this relationship, and we were not any closer to each other. *Is it me? Do I have commitment issues? Why won't God bless this union? I thought we were meant for each other. We've struggled five years to make this relationship work. Surely that proves our commitment to each other. After all this, shouldn't we be able to go through anything in life together?*

I opened the door, stepped out of my car, and hardly even noticed the weight burdening my shoulders as I walked. I'd grown accustomed to the constant baggage. The scars of the fight to keep it all going were like second nature to me.

I walked into the care pastor's office and explained everything, laying all my secrets out on the table. I explained how I came from the commercial sex industry and how my fiancé still worked in the business. How the more I wanted him to leave, the more he pursued one more deal to make more money. How I understood the need to provide but not at the expense of our family.

How there was no way I was raising a family with one of us still involved in the porn business. I never wanted our children to hear some of the comments he made toward me or other women. "Is it fair for me to ask him to leave?" I asked, before continuing to process in circles around myself. "After all, we both worked in the business– that's where we met."

I told the pastor that Dru was also addicted to pain pills and the medications the doctors gave him to get off those, such as Suboxone. That all he wanted to do was sleep. That some days, he would say things, such as, "Wow, I thought I'd die last night!" I wanted the person I married to have the will to live. I didn't want our kids or me to wake up one morning and find that he had overdosed. "How," I asked, "am I supposed to marry someone I don't know will live much longer if he keeps doing this to himself?" I nearly shouted this question, now thoroughly worked up and deeply distressed.

The pastor waited for a moment, his presence like an unmoved island in the midst of a churning sea. Then he spoke, and I instantly knew his words were my direct answer from God. He proceeded to tell me how a godly man would cherish and value me. "If you were with a godly man, you would not be afraid that he would hurt you or make demands that you could not fulfill. He would not keep bringing up your past or put you down by saying things such as, 'I don't need sex from you. I'll take care of myself.'" He said that in a godly marriage, the couple can freely give their bodies to each other without guarding themselves selfishly.

His perceptive gaze locked on my face, and he remarked aloud, "By the glossed-over look in your eyes when I said the word 'cherished,' I can tell you have never felt truly loved, cherished, or valued." Wordless, I could only stare back in return. He handed me the book *Captivating* by John and Stasi Eldredge, and said, "It's okay to long to be cherished." As if my arm were independent of my body, it stretched out to take the book. It was a surreal moment yet more real than so many moments of my life. Then he gave me the number of a potential female mentor who attended church there for follow up and gently closed our conversation. Amazed, relieved, in shock yet resolved, I went home with my answer. I now knew that I wanted to trust God fully in our relationship. To do that, I would have to find a new way to relate to Dru and break off the sexual part of our relationship until we were married.

I had been going to church long enough to know that my relationship as it stood was breaking the heart of God. What Father would want to see his children hurt like that? How could I ask God to bless something that was destroying both Dru and me and preventing us from getting the help we needed individually? Ever since I got sober, Dru had become my higher power. Instead of God as the ultimate authority in our relationship, I had put Dru on the highest altar and asked him to protect my heart when he had no means or tools to do so. I was expecting him to be someone he wasn't yet. He did not understand the most intimate part of my life, my relationship with the true God. All at once, I could see clearly. It was time for me to choose: Dru or God.

I wrote Dru a letter and told him that I wanted to present a right relationship before God if we were to ever have a wedding day. One that made God first and honored him in all we said and did. He didn't speak to me for a couple days, but after talking with his new friends at the few church planting meetings he had attended with me, he realized the next step was for me to move out. It would have been a great way for us to get to know each other with boundaries, only he was so cold and distant during the process, we never had a real chance.

This move was supposed to be something we did together in anticipation of what God would do when we offered up our entire beings to him. But instead of joyfully experiencing the process with me, Dru became even more disrespectful in fear of losing me for good. He disappeared the day I moved out. People from church came on a Saturday and helped me move all the gym equipment and mirrors into a storefront property in my name. While I was setting up my now-public business so that it was ready by the start of the work week, the church planting team was busy moving my half of the house into a room at a friend's where I would stay until I got on my feet. It was like getting a divorce. I did not feel as if we would grow closer together but rather felt a separation that was cold and bone-chilling.

We barely talked for the next couple of weeks except to handle the credit cards that were in both of our names. Then finally it hit me. We were finally done for good. We had nothing left to give each other. I couldn't expect someone to honor me when he wasn't sure of his own faith and didn't yet have the same values I did. We had officially grown apart.

With one text message, it was over for good. The afternoon we broke up, I finished my volunteer commitment at church and headed over to the martial arts studio. I had picked up the hobby of martial arts a year earlier to distract me from my addictions and to channel my energy into something productive. I was testing for my orange belt, and it was the perfect night to do so. I did great, and with passing that test, I moved on to the next season of my life. I began training as a potential instructor at the studio and started preparing to get involved in some professional kickboxing tournaments. I was training an average of once or twice a day, up to fourteen times a week.

Outside of that, I began operating my own gym—a gym that I spent thousands of dollars to get up and running in less than a week. Clients started coming in, and God seemed to be blessing what little I was faithful to offer up by adding more. I began networking and became involved in various community organizations. I also became the chairperson of some major community events. I was busy by day and heartbroken by night. But I would not allow myself to feel the pain. It was time to move forward. I was free from the sex industry and all that had been holding me back. I ignored anything that didn't have to do with my new work.

I met with the female mentor I was referred to and asked to be considered as a mentor for other women. She kindly responded that now was my time to grow in my relationship with God before I was ready to take on a new role. *What does that mean?* I wanted to ask. I'd just had my heart broken and was doing everything I thought God had asked of me. How much longer did I need to wait before I could put my pain to a greater purpose? My mentor gave me the number to an outside ministry, a support group for those leaving the industry started by some former sex workers. She reiterated, "Deanna, this is for *you* to get help, not to give help." She was right. Though I was volunteering with many causes, I'd refused to seek the help that *I* needed. Still, I didn't call.

Even the church launch team began to reach out and talk to me about starting the process of healing. They loved having me on the team but could see I was on the verge of breaking down, maybe for good.

SAME STORY, DIFFERENT RELAPSE

On September 1, 2011, I turned twenty-eight. Summer was nearly over, and this was the first birthday in five years that I wasn't celebrating with Dru. My friend, Jen, one of the leaders of the church plant, met me at church and asked how I was doing. I started to tell her about all the things I was busy with. She stopped me: "No, I want to know how *you* are doing." People found it strange that I refused to talk about my breakup. But then, while I was sitting across the table from her, I unexpectedly received a text from Dru, saying, "Happy birthday." And that was it. I fell apart.

I told her I had nothing in me anymore. Dru's brother-in-law and sister were well, Dru seemed to be well, and I felt as if I were drowning in pain. I felt as if God didn't need me anymore. After all, I thought I was responsible to help everyone, and they all seemed healthier when I left their lives. She started to cry as I lay there, sobbing uncontrollably and hyperventilating.

"That is a lie from the devil!" she declared.

In pure agony, I choked out, "I have nothing left!"

She encouraged me then to let myself feel the pain. I couldn't gather the strength to lift my head off the table, so I just wept until I couldn't anymore. Then I canceled all my clients and my volunteer work for the day, went home, and rested. I was exhausted from trying to keep my head above water on my own when God had never asked that of me. In fact, he promised to be with me in the water if I would trust him.

I made my next choice, half-blinded by numbness, half-able to see only my pain. I went to the ministry for those leaving the sex industry, which I'd been encouraged to attend a few days earlier. At the first meeting, the topic was intimacy. But I had no idea what intimacy was, so I cried in frustration. I knew what porn sex was, and that was about it. I had no idea that intimacy was not merely physical. Intimacy was what made the physical such a gift: It was

159

oneness with someone. I had never heard such a powerful concept. I couldn't handle how uncomfortable this idea made me. I realized that everything I had believed about love and sex was a lie. I would have to relearn *everything,* starting from the ground up. Everyone around me sat there and listened, but none of us had any answers. We were present, absorbing the information. After two or three more weekly, one-hour meetings, I had so many wounds opened up that I wondered how I was supposed to begin to heal, let alone go back and face life.

The pain of my past work in the industry and past relationships resulted in paranoia and PTSD. I became paranoid that people in my life knew who I was and knew about the career choices I had made. It turned out that quite a few of them *did* know. People in my new business circles were talking about it. My clients were finding old videos and more on the internet. Fans even posted my real name and related information on the adult sites. Whenever a normal guy did seem interested, I wondered, *Is he interested in me or in* her?

The pain of my past work in the industry and past relationships resulted in paranoia and PTSD.

"Who is '*she*'?" asked Debbie, a new mentor Jen had arranged for me. She was different. She didn't want to fix me; she wanted to walk with me through my pain. She lived in Kentucky, but she flew down for weeks at a time and made sure to stay close to me. She said, "Deanna, that was you—*she* was you—and God loved you even when you were doing those things. It hurt him, because it was hurting you, but he still loved you. And you need to process that deeply." I sat glued to the high-top chair in the church coffee house as I listened, in awe of what she had just said. She told me that God was "jealous for me" in a good way, not in a controlling way. He waited patiently to be my refuge once I was ready to stop running in circles. Then she said she knew a place where girls who came out of the industry could receive healing. I said, "Great! I know some women who could use that!" Once again, I was ignoring my own pain. She didn't push.

Back at my weekly meeting, I felt someone—I knew it was the devil—whisper in my ear, "Aren't you tired of trying to be good? Haven't you tried long enough?" I'd had about three months of sexual purity by that point and was exhausted from trying to live the life that was supposed to bring me freedom. If that were the case, why did I feel so horrible? I told my group I was going to call Brad, who I had met at a Chamber of Commerce event, for a hook up. He seemed interested. I left my group with these words, "I'm sorry. It's the best I can do. I need some attention from a man."

I took out the bikini I had stashed in my glove box in case Brad invited me for a late night swim. I went to his place, already premeditating relapse of my sexual standards. After the swim, I went to his apartment and spent the night. He and I didn't go all the way, so I was proud of myself. *Maybe I can do this*, I thought. Debbie told me that I was playing with fire, though—and I was.

Within one month, the relationship I'd been building with my friend-turned-roommate was now all but gone. So I gave her space, and I moved in with one of my newest clients. I began to work at a bar on the weekends, still calling my sponsor and telling her every honest detail. I continued to push the limits with Brad, thinking, *Well, since he's not in the industry, maybe he is a step up.* He even went to church with me. He had a little boy whom I loved playing games with, and we went to these fantastic charity events together. I thought these were great improvements over my previous relationships.

The problem was, he had no boundaries. He put his hand way up high on my leg under the table at dinner and way low on my back when we went out. All this was on our first date. I never knew whether I was uncomfortable or flattered when he did those things. I thought, *Maybe this is how normal people date.* His signals gave me enough assurance that I knew I could turn to him when I needed some attention.

He was also very emotionally unstable and went through major times of depression while we were together. My new housemate, Genie, took it upon herself to get him out of these funks. I'd come home, and they'd be getting ready to go to parties together—parties that I was not invited to. They would drink together on the couch while I hid out in my room, frustrated because he had asked me to not be affectionate with him in front to her. He had said it would make her sad. What was this? How had I ended up being another man's secret girl?

Genie, Brad, and I all attended the same networking parties. I'd dress up, hoping he'd be there on behalf of his company. I planned to make sure he noticed me. Only everyone in the room would talk to me except him. He found it more appropriate to spend the evening with Genie in public. Then he called at the end of the night to tell me how beautiful I looked and how intimidated he was to talk to me. I wasn't buying a word of it.

Needless to say, I wrote him off about once every other week just as I had done in past relationships. At the same time, Dru and I were now trying to be friends—ever since he had called me on my birthday. He brought me oatmeal at work, and we met up once at a Halloween event at the new church launch. I discovered that evening that he was on just enough pain meds to get him through the night. We went to stay at his sister's house since she lived nearby. She and her husband had been attending since the launch, and I was happy to go to church with them. They even gave us separate rooms to sleep in to help us honor our new values. He nodded out from the pills like old times, and I slipped into my room. I thought, *Why am I even bothering with him?* The next day, he ignored me, and then we began fighting on and off because of a text he misinterpreted. He and I continued this pattern for a week, but then we both gave up on the friendship. We were done playing these games.

PARANOIA

By now, Brad and I were sleeping together regularly. I told my friends at church that I had done the best I could. They knew that this was not what I wanted in my heart of hearts; I just didn't know how to break this pattern. Suicide was once again looking like an attractive option. I fought these dark thoughts by showing Brad pictures of Tiana, hoping he would want to be with someone who looked like that. Then, in my despair over bringing Tiana out of hiding, I told the devil he'd won. I had no cards left to play.

I often discovered Brad's car at my house when I hadn't been there. He'd been alone with Genie too many times. Each time, I pictured them having orgies while I was away and laughing behind my back at how dumb I was. These were not the only thoughts I battled daily. I also went out with couples after work, and I prepared myself for when, with a few subtle hints, they'd invite me to join their relationship—like the swingers I used to live with. Where I lived, these types of three-way relationships in marriage were becoming so prevalent, they were even the topic of a church sermon two weekends later.

In the midst of this paranoia, I knew only misery. Every night, when I took a bath, suicidal thoughts would flood my mind. I could no longer recognize what was true of myself, my life, humanity, or even of God. I realized I need help. My thinking was filtered through my childhood and what I had been taught in ten years of work in the sex industry. Some of the negative thoughts I perceived may have been true, but I desperately needed to see some good. All I could see was a world full of people using each other for sex. I saw relationships and myself through the eyes of porn. I didn't know if I was ashamed or proud of my past. But with a dark certainty, I *did* know that if I didn't get to the root of my problems, I would end up in jail, in a mental institution, or dead. I had to do something. But what?

I hit my knees, threw up my hands, and screamed at God, *"What do you want from me?*

CHAPTER SEVENTEEN

REFUGE

HERE I WAS, finally at my end, face down on my kitchen floor, terrified of what was next. Little did I know I was kneeling at the entrance of a new season that would bring me *real* life. When we come to the end of ourselves, God shows up to meet us there. That's often the first time we are willing to listen. He never leaves; he never taunts us by refusing to speak. But it's hard to hear him when we are consumed with ourselves.

But this day, I was consumed only with the desire to surrender—to receive a word, a direction, a lifeline from God. I was *desperate* to hear him speak. And so I waited in the silence created after the echo of my own broken question had faded. I was still on my knees in the kitchen when I received a text message from my dear friend, Jen, from Mission Church. "I think you should really pray about that house in Kentucky that Debbie suggested to you." I suddenly remembered Debbie's words about this place: it was the ministry where she had said I could truly rest and recover, the same place I thought offered hope for others but not for me. At first, I fought her words and encouragement.

"What about the business I just opened? What about the life I've built here?" I protested.

She was very honest in her response, choosing in that moment not to mince words. With loving directness, she boldly declared that I was barely making a living, and I certainly wasn't making a life. Debt was accumulating faster than I could pay it back. I was drowning my sorrows in new clothes, shoes, purses, fancy events, and restaurants, because I told myself I deserved it for all the great decisions I was making. In the quick moment it took to take honest stock of my own life, I realized she was right. Any further protests faded away.

And as I embraced the truth of her words, peace enveloped me, like the warm hug of a weighted blanket. A voice inside whispered with quiet certainty, *I am going to Kentucky.* I called my sponsor, who had been watching me disappear and take one wrong path after another throughout my sobriety. I asked what she thought about this decision. "Am I just running again?" I asked, genuinely wanting to make sure one way or the other. By now, I sincerely trusted her to help me process my thoughts and plans.

She said, "Deanna, I don't think that you are running away. I honestly think this time, you are running *toward* something. I have been praying for a place just like this that would help you in this terribly painful area of your life." As her words sunk in, I could feel that something bigger was happening here. A place of hope exploded inside me—wide and spacious, like a field ready to be plowed and planted. Healing was awaiting me in a house many states away.

I reached out to make contact with the ministry, Refuge For Women, in Kentucky. I discovered they were a non-profit, faith-based organization that provided specialized long-term care for women who have escaped human trafficking or sexual exploitation. Women could live in the safe house for up to twelve months free of charge. Twelve months without having to fight to survive! They had around-the-clock care and focused evidence-based, trauma-informed curriculum. Refuge for Women had one desire: to help each woman like me complete the program with a vision for her future, equipped to succeed and sustain a life marked with dignity and hope.

Dignity and hope. It was a bold mission, a beautiful promise, and a life that I could hardly dream of. But as was typical for me, as I glimpsed hope for the future, I began to doubt. The house in Kentucky was specifically for women leaving prostitution, escorting, stripping, and pornography, but I had been out of the industry for almost two years. What if they didn't deem my situation an emergency? I didn't need rescuing; I needed renewing. Or so I told myself.

But something deep inside me must have known: I was actually in much need of rescuing. Desperate and exhausted, I called the executive director of the ministry. I pleaded with him and told him that if this didn't work, I had no other options. I didn't need another rehab; I'd had a wealth of people to help me stay sober these past few years. I didn't need another institution either. I needed a break from my trauma, a safe place to unpack and heal so I could finally stop the inevitable cycle of adding to it. When he amazingly agreed that I should come, my course was finally set—toward *life*, in all its fullness.

I remembered again what my mentor had told me. "When you are ready to stop running in circles, I know a place where you can find rest."

What an amazing word: "rest." I'd spent an entire lifetime in survival mode. When I finally left a life of selling sex, I set out right away on an adventure to prove to the world what I could do. I was tired, and my efforts were fleeting. I kept building up myself and my life with all these events and accomplishments, only to later find myself in a puddle of tears—sick to my stomach—lonely, ashamed, and still feeling unworthy and hopeless.

I needed a break from my trauma, a safe place to unpack and heal so I could finally stop the inevitable cycle of adding to it.

I'd reached out to many places that said they helped people in the XXX industry, yet none of them could offer me the direction I needed to start over. Many organizations prayed with me to get out of the industry, but when I was out, I had no one to provide me with resources on how to manage life emotionally. Nearly everyone I had ever met had used or abused me. How could I trust that it wouldn't happen again?

I didn't understand how to navigate finances in my new life either. This was a huge issue as I had been making over $100,000 a year (which is not common in the industry anymore), and suddenly, all that money had stopped. My bills reflected my former income, but I now had no way to keep up with them. I was lacking the basic life skills to help me have self-control and spend responsibly. Ultimately, getting out of the industry had just unveiled a new set of problems. I had to stand on my own two feet and keep up with the car payments, rent, and credit card bills that reflected my lavish lifestyle, all while trying to deal with the emotional trauma that kept surfacing in my relationships and nightmares.

But finally, there was a solution: this home in Kentucky with beds to house a handful of women who wanted a new life. I didn't have to figure out how to get my life together on my own. Someone would help me start from scratch. From offering legal help to providing for my basic needs for one year to being given the chance to live in a quiet location where God's voice would finally be the loudest, this place had me covered. I truly could feel my heart panting, desperately thirsty for a drink from a deep well, at the idea of this kind of rest. (See Psalm 42:1 and John 7:37–39.)

I called my parents and told them they wouldn't be hearing from me for at least six months, possibly a whole year. This was not a Refuge requirement, but *I* needed to silence all the voices in my life. I also made a choice to unplug my computer and phone so that I would have no distractions on this journey to healing. My friends and family started to panic, asking questions about what sort of degrees these people had who were going to help me. They were fixated on the tangible, but I knew better. I had been to many different counselors since I was a young child, and I even tried therapies to supposedly heal my brain from everything I had experienced in life. While seeking help from these individuals had led to a few positive results, I'd had no permanent relief, no actual or lasting freedom. This place offered me a chance to lay it all down and come out as a healthy, grounded, and whole person.

I stayed a few nights with a friend and her family, who were truly angels to me, until I could go. We went through my storage units together, and I gave away all the gym equipment. This life that I'd built needed to be narrowed down to two suitcases—all that was allotted me to take to the safe house in Kentucky. Before I could talk myself out of it, we made three quick piles: a Goodwill pile, a pile of memorabilia for my parents to store in Arizona, and the pile that I would take on my new journey.

Once all was said and done, I went to say my goodbyes. I had one last meeting with my life group, and these words jumped off a mug that had been gifted in the Christmas exchange. "For I know the plans I have for you," declares the Lord, 'plans to prosper you and not to harm you, plans to give you hope and a future'" (Jeremiah 29:11 NIV). I told everyone, "Those words are for me! I am hanging on to this promise!" And I meant it.

My friends walked with me through all the pain I was experiencing and hung around even when I slipped back into old sexual habits one final time. I found my way back to Brad, like an addict before rehab who drinks every last drop in her liquor cabinet, knowing she can never do so again. This was an attempt to numb my emotions and calm my fears and to prove I was beyond help. They stood by me as I crawled to the door of freedom inch by inch. But after that final night, I woke up the next day and left him for good. No turning back now. I dropped off my car for voluntary repossession. This was the last painful material item I had needed to let go of since I would not be able to afford a $650 car payment in Kentucky.

The lyrics of "You're Not Shaken" by Phil Stacey were the last words I heard before I jumped in my friend's car and headed toward my new life. I may have been shaken—many times in my life, even the previous night—but I knew my God wasn't. I just had to hang on because I knew, in the depths of my being, that my life was about to take an amazing turn.

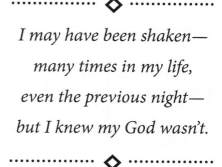

I may have been shaken— many times in my life, even the previous night— but I knew my God wasn't.

My new life officially began when I drove away from everything I'd known and toward a state I'd never seen with my temporary family of angels. As we headed down the freeway straight for LAX, I saw him—Dru—one last time. The very truck I'd asked him to buy because it was my favorite flashed by, and I saw him through the window. But as soon as I'd glimpsed him, he was gone. He pulled off the freeway out of my line of sight.

The experience was both a literal and symbolic representation of our journeys down two separate paths.

I boarded the plane with two bags of my most expensive clothes. I might be moving to Kentucky, far from the lights and red carpets of California, but that wouldn't stop me from bringing the nicest clothes I owned. I'd worked hard for those. They were, in a small way, both a comfort and a symbol of confidence for me. Stowing them carefully above me, I settled in for my literal, and ironically longer-than-expected, flight to freedom. Twelve hours later, after two flights and several delays, my mentor Debbie was there to meet me with a friend in tow—a girl who was about to become the sister of support and encouragement I had always longed for. It was finally happening. God was building a family for me. One where I was not a burden.

Upon my arrival at the Refuge For Women house, a beautiful poster decorated by the other residents with the words, "Welcome Home," was taped on the front door. Immediately, relief flooded over me. The mere sight of the word "home" brought such joy to my heart. I was so happy to be free and safe that it nearly freaked the other girls out. They didn't understand why I was so peaceful and happy. But I understood my own reaction perfectly: It was because I knew my old life would finally be behind me. I would no longer have to sell myself in every way imaginable just to get by. I wouldn't need to expose myself to the lies of this world, repeated to me relentlessly through TV, radio, or bad relationships. For the next year, I could focus solely on God and his plan for my life—plans for my good and the good of those around me.

As my eyes drank in the sight of my new home, my gaze was drawn to lettering above the dining table. On the wall, Jeremiah 29:11 was painted in beautifully scripted letters: "For I know the plans I have for you." My heart thrilled at the discovery of this small but incredibly meaningful surprise. I knew logically it had been painted up there long ago without me specifically in mind, but in that private moment, I was delighted to know it had ended up there with *exactly* me in mind. Smiling genuinely and sighing with contentment, I took it as confirmation that I was in the right place. Once again, God had met me where I was. And now, he would journey on with me into the healing and the future that had been just out of reach for so long.

CHAPTER EIGHTEEN

SET FREE

AFTER MY INITIAL EXCITEMENT wore off, I went into mental shock from all the drastic changes that I'd made in just a week. It was the day after I arrived and only two days before Christmas. I loved holidays, but I couldn't even acknowledge, let alone process, Christmas that year. Deep, buried, and lifelong pain began to surface, and I needed to face it head on. I wasn't ready to celebrate anything in my life. I only wanted to find out how, at twenty-eight years old, I had ended up in a safe house screaming for help while life was passing me by.

Debbie asked me if I needed anything, and I said, "No, I have everything I need in Jesus." Genuine though I desired this statement to be, it was instead proof that I had swung from one extreme to another: from caring intensely about material things to denying my own actual needs. While Jesus is, of course, both good and utterly sufficient for the deepest needs we face, even he understands basic human needs. When I could deny it no longer, I admitted my humanity was screaming for a physical jacket. I had grown up in the desert before moving to the beach; I had no winter clothes. Nothing in the two bags of expensive clothing I'd brought along was holding up to the Kentucky cold. So I asked Debbie for a jacket, and she gifted me above and beyond my small request, making sure I had a scarf, earmuffs, mittens, and an electric blanket too.

Once my outsides were warm, it was time to thaw the insides. So I grabbed every book available to be very proactive with my healing. There was no time like the present! I opened a devotional book and read Psalm 46:10: "Cease striving and know that I am God"(NASB). Well, it didn't get any clearer than that—God had a work to do. A work that required my participation but not my achievement.

The theme of being still and letting go continued to surface. I showed up to my one-on-one time one day, and Ked asked, "Deanna, why do you wear all this stuff?"

"What stuff?" I responded in confusion.

"All your diamond jewelry, rhinestones on your Couture outfits, Louis Vuitton on your belt buckle, Dior written across your bags, and sunglasses. What are you covering up?"

At first, I didn't really understand his question. But before I knew what was happening, I proceeded to tell him that all this stuff was everything I had to show for what I did in the industry. "If I didn't have these things, everything I went through was all for nothing." As I spoke these words out loud, another conversation was happening inside my head. My own voice was taunting me. These words looped over and over in my mind like an audio file stuck on repeat, until I screamed out loud, *"It was all for nothing!"*

As I released my tortured admission, the dam of my own denial cracked open inside me, freeing the torrents of pain and brokenness it had held at bay. I began wailing so loudly, the entire house downstairs could hear me. And in that moment, I decided I wanted none of it: none of the fake image that made me look as if everything were okay on the outside when everything was horrible on the inside. I no longer wanted to attract attention to my appearance only to draw it away from my true self. No more image management for me.

This new decision included even more intensive healing work by getting two eating disorders under control. I had been an anorexic during the week, but then I binged on the weekends. As a health professional, I thought I had learned how to supplement and justify having a maximum of five hundred calories per day. But this self-deception also came into the light, and I dealt with the lies I believed about myself that had built up over the years. The most recent version of my false self was shaped by the fitness industry, which had taught me life was all about me and how I looked. My younger self would have said I didn't have enough worth to deserve eating. But once I was successful and beautiful and *did* deserve to eat, the very same lie— still playing like a tape in my head—led me to stuff myself sick. Feeling that I deserved food was a fleeting conviction, too, and so I'd found myself vacillating between unhealthy extremes. To make it all worse, my experience in the porn industry had left me with memories of watching as my 105-pound self was airbrushed for magazine and movie covers. I had watched every detail that they altered, and so I knew where all my flaws were. I had felt huge and disgusting for so long. But now, I finally realized it was time for me to stop shopping in the junior section and become comfortable as a grown woman.

I let go of the two suitcases of stuff I had brought, and the church in Kentucky fixed me up with some practical clothes. I started to discover what it was like to be comfortable in my own skin. No more flashy clothes, tanning, painting my face, and dying my hair. Not that any of those things are bad, in and of themselves, but in that season, they were bad for me. *I* needed to know what it felt like to not hide behind these things. As I continued the daily practice of stripping away the fake self and the fancy look, for the first time in my life, I began to feel beautiful. I looked in the mirror, and I could now see myself the way that God saw me. No more striving to *become* what I thought was required of me; now, I was just *being* me.

> *To make it all worse, my experience in the porn industry had left me with memories of watching as my 105-pound self was airbrushed for magazine and movie covers.*
> *I had watched every detail that they altered, and so I knew where all my flaws were.*

As I started to become more comfortable with my external appearance, a deep knowledge grew within me that this wasn't the only surrender I needed to make. I knew seeing myself differently was not the only reason I was here. So I dove in and committed to more hard work. I spent months learning healthy boundaries and God's design for all types of relationships. I made many mistakes as I navigated what healthy was, but the more I surrendered, the more God was filling me up with wisdom and with peace. His voice was now telling me which way to go. I learned that not all people are healthy, and not everyone needed to be in my inner circle. This was an important transformation from the way I used to think, which was that transparency meant letting *everyone* in. Instead, now I could appreciate where I was in my journey and where others were and make appropriate decisions about investing in relationships based on that. I learned to trust my own instincts. And when I had questions, I had a network of support who could offer their experience.

Within this network, numerous people held me accountable to my healing journey and ultimately helped dissolve the long-term unhealthy connection between Dru and I. They side-tracked letters, intercepted phone calls, and mediated for the next two years. They knew this would help at least one of us to heal but held out genuine hope that both of us would find freedom. We had been addicted to the drama of toxicity, but we called it passion. We were jealous and crazy and called it love.

"Love . . . " I breathed out the word slowly as the beginning of a prayer one day. I was so tired but still filled with longing to delve deeper and really know true love. "Lord, help me to know love." I did not want to go back to California or back to Dru until we were both capable of true, God-honoring, selfless love.

Since those were my new boundaries for our relationship, I now realized I had to be honest with myself; it didn't look like a relationship with Dru would happen. Over and over and *over* again, I had to grieve the pain of our lost relationship and its non-existent future. I had to grieve the death of a dream—what that relationship could never be. That relationship had been everything to me. Just when I thought I was done uprooting the deepest connections, I found more I needed to deal with. And in this, I discovered I wasn't alone. All the girls in the house seemed to struggle with this same issue. We each had that one person—one toxic relationship that we had allowed to become our everything. Some of the other girls left their programs and went back to that toxic relationship. Without massive help and support, a fierce resolve to persist in healing, and a strong commitment to God and to myself, I would have done the same.

But thank God, I did have that support. And I *was* fundamentally convinced that I needed a greater love—one that would fill me up so much that a distorted love like the one I'd shared with Dru would never again look like an attractive option. I fervently prayed for God to help me to grasp his love. I set up weekly dates with Jesus, and I met him in special, secret places: out by the creek or in a favorite tree. I would climb up and sit among the branches, and I'd wait patiently to hear him speak to my heart. I showed up, still and quiet, and simply allowed him to embrace me with his presence. He promised through his Word that if I sought him, I would always find him, and I learned that he kept his promises. I sought, and I found. (See Jeremiah 29:13.) And I fell deeper and deeper into a love that was filling me up in all the right ways.

Curiosity compelled me to pursue this love further. On Easter Weekend, I watched *The Passion of the Christ*. The movie was graphic and hard to handle, but I was desperate to grasp exactly what Christ had done for me and why. As the movie closed, I was overwhelmed with anger and pain yet a fierce gratitude in the core of my being. I walked out of the room, knowing with everything within me, that this was the ultimate love, and I could stop searching. "No man will ever love me as much as Jesus does. I will never again settle for less than a selfless love that brings me closer to him." Then I stayed silent for a while, letting the profound truth wash over me. I was rocked gently in waves of his presence, his pleasure, and his peace. After sitting with the revelation for a time, I called my mentor and asked, "What do you think about me getting baptized again?" She told me she had already felt a nudge in her spirit that I would be asking about this.

My first baptism still marked my choice to declare acceptance of the finished work of Jesus: I was already saved for eternity by putting my faith in him rather than in myself. But I had a beautiful friend in recovery who once said, "The first time I was baptized, Jesus offered himself to me just as I was. The second time I was baptized, I offered myself to him." And these words struck a chord deep within my heart. I wanted to publicly and worshipfully offer all of myself to God.

So that was exactly what I did. I'd found the one I knew for certain I would follow for the rest of my life. No turning back. As I planned this day, I invited a few close people to be in the waters with me. Those by my side in the pond were like bridesmaids at a wedding. They were people I had entrusted on this journey to help remind me of my commitment to Christ when life grew hard, just as matrimonial attendants are meant to help a married couple remember their commitment to God and to their covenant relationship in hard times. These women stood with me, agreeing to uphold my commitment and adding to my joy.

On the ride to the pond where I was baptized, I listened to a song by Matt Redman, called *Never Once*. In it, he sings about how Jesus is always with us during the journey. As the lyrics washed over me, I had no doubt it was true. *I might have walked away multiple times, but I knew the whole time that Jesus never left me.* He was waiting for me to turn to him instead of to everyone and anything else. To commemorate my baptism, the church gave me a T-shirt that said, "Set Free." Before I knew I was forgiven; but I had never known I could be free. But here and now—this was truly free.

Before my baptism, I'd gone about life all wrong. I had thought I needed to live right to be worthy, clean, or good. I tried to stay good by my own will and in my own strength, because it was what I was supposed to do. But I failed miserably. I wanted to follow the rules. But if I slipped up and didn't, religious people told me my ways were wrong, without the heart or knowledge to show me how to live a godly life.

But The Refuge gave me a place to learn this and eventually to help others do the same. I discovered that fruit comes with this new kind of life—a fruit that encompasses love, joy, peace, patience, kindness, gentleness, goodness, faithfulness, and self-control (Galatians 5:22–23 NASB). No matter how hard I had tried before, I could never manufacture a life that evidenced that fruit on my own. I needed a power greater than myself, a power that operated in love. At the Refuge for Women, I learned not only how to recognize this love, but also how to abide in it. I learned how to enter into love, become transformed, and grow beautiful, vibrant, fruit. Unconditional love—both the love of God and the love of others—finally set me free for good.

CHAPTER NINETEEN

FINISHING THE RACE

ALL YEAR, I'd been experiencing the reality that freedom happens layer by layer. Now, I was healthier, more whole, and more fully myself than I'd ever been. And I was reaching the end of my journey with the Refuge for Women. It was time to unravel one final layer—time to return to a key place of pain and deception in my old life. By now, I had banked a few victories and was ready to reclaim some ground that had been taken from me. I was learning that God doesn't leave us where we are. He continues to transform us and equip us for greater things if we will allow him to. He longs to give us back what the enemy tried to steal, kill, and destroy. (See John 10:10.) And so with much prayer and training to prepare me, I knew it was the right time for me to go back to Vegas.

The war for my future was not my battle to fight, but I had a role to play. I had to stay close to my community of support and hang tightly to these words: "I will repay you for the years the locusts have eaten . . . You will have plenty to eat, until you are full, and you will praise the name of the Lord your God, who has worked wonders for you; never again will my people be shamed" (Joel 2:25–26 NIV). Emboldened by the truths of

Scripture throughout my journey, I truly had thrown off every weight that was holding me back so that I could run the race set before me. (See Hebrews

12:1–2.) And now, my return to Vegas was for a *literal* race. In fact, I had been training for this physical race throughout my year of holistic recovery. This was an embodied, capstone event for my healing journey. And I was confident that every physical mile gained would also represent a new spiritual victory for me.

The second we landed and went to pick up our race packets, the battle began. Of course, the race packets would have to be in the same hotel where the AVN show was formerly held each year. This was the place where hundreds of people had shown up, grabbed me, and left with autographed DVDs, capturing my most traumatizing and humiliating moments ever. It was the place that celebrated with awards movies, where I was drunk or high in order to tolerate the pain of filming such degrading scenes. I was back here, in that place. Only this time, no one was grabbing or following me. This time, I wasn't met with alcohol to rid me of the shakes and prepare me to step into character. I had no more character. No more reason to escape. Now I saw life differently. I saw the glazed-over looks on people's faces as they gambled away their weekend. I saw the naked girls on the mass-produced cards left all over the sidewalks; these were real people to me, real people with hearts. Real people who call me to this day, wondering if they will ever be able to leave life in the brothel behind.

> *The place was no different than before, but I was. I never thought change like that would be possible.*

In this familiar—but now so different—place, I was momentarily overwhelmed by the onslaught of data assaulting my senses from a new perspective mixed with old memories. But then I gained my composure and captured the moment by writing a poem.

> Bells, whistles, and lights everywhere,
> the smell of cigars and liquor fill the air.
> So many times I was here without a care,
> not knowing each time, my heart would eventually tear.

I walk down the strip and can't help but smile,
at the schemes of the devil; not one was worthwhile!
I stroll down the Venetian, and it becomes very clear,
none of this is funny; I was holding back tears.

Music is blaring; it all sounds the same.
Only today I'm me; I'm signing my real name.
How could I not see this all was a game?
That all of it was a false fame!
All over the world, to this one room fans came.
Only now I see the façade that was lame,
and ouch, my heart feels the years it was maimed!
"Let's take a picture," they'd say, and it all set in:
the overwhelming pain of my sin.

I curl up on the stairs where I used to take my breaks,
I let the tears pour out as my body shakes.
I'm so done with the lies; I'm done being fake.
I get down on my knees for my God's sake.

To offer him a soul-deep plea, a cry from my heart;
no longer do I need to let Vegas memories tear me apart.

First I had to renounce every autograph, every lie,
every marriage, every heart, that porn caused to die.
My spirit trembles as I lay there and sigh,
now seeing the truth, asking myself why?

Why did I allow the lie to go this deep,
only to be haunted for years in my sleep?
But cheerfully I gave my heart to Jesus to keep,
the *only* one who gave me a harvest of freedom to reap.

I walk back out with my head held up high,
knowing there's a heartfelt tear in each eye.
I'm done with the mask; it's okay to cry;
I'll walk in my new self. His commands I'll apply.

I'm ready for the picture, "Everyone say cheese!"

I left with new memories, and my heart was pleased.
I missed the show, but the reclaiming was done,
for the God who loved me so much and gave me his Son.

The people I love, the lies make me irate,
so I will go out and lead my friends to the gate.
The gate of love they cannot be separated from,
if only they share in my joy, accept him, and come.

This is the day and here is that hour
that God restored what the locust devoured.

Despite the final moments of pain during this encounter, I honestly did feel restored. And I felt deeply thankful, too, that running a race was not my only purpose in Vegas. In the few short hours we were there, I was already a changed woman. The place was no different than before, but I was. I never thought change like that would be possible. But here I had lived it for myself, and I was humbled by it all.

I had already experienced much emotional healing, so I was feeling much lighter for all that still lay ahead of me on this trip. Practically, I still had a race to run, so I loaded up on carbs. And then in she walked: Jen from Mission Church. She was not about to let me run this race without her. I found out that one year ago, right here, she and Ked ran this race and prayed for me. This was only weeks before I had fallen to my knees and texted her. My heart was overwhelmed with the fact that in the very moments I didn't feel my life was worth fighting for, other people did, and they proved it in both their words and actions. Now here I was, with a life worth living, ready to both physically and metaphorically finish my race and fight to the finish. All the while, I could pray for the many others I knew were still trapped in the darkness of my own former life—that they, too, would find renewed strength and hope for a new future.

When the race began, I took off, and my tribe ran with me. We all stayed together, excited to make our way toward this monumental finish line. But fueled as we were with hope and exhilaration, after three miles we still had to stop running, catch a breath, and pace ourselves. The rest of the race was full of stops and starts. Some moments, I wondered, *Is it worth it? Did I make a mistake signing up for this?* Not even in those moments was I left alone in my struggle and self-doubt. At one point, I'd pulled off to the side, and Jen, my greatest cheerleader, was ready with encouragement.

"Whatever you do, Deanna, don't stop moving!" She exclaimed, her smile stretched wide and eyes overflowed with enthusiasm and light.

I was in so much physical pain that I only wanted to curl up on the side of the road. I felt positive that I couldn't take another step. But then I told myself, *No, this isn't even about me anymore. It is about the millions of women out there who have lost their strength.* This year, I had been in the race of my life, and now I was here, praying for others to begin their own race. My life now was filled with purpose beyond living for myself. I had to keep going.

I looked at the love-filled and encouraging face of my friend Jen, and I pushed my body to give me more. "I'm ready," I told my cheerleader. "Let's go." We'd jog a few steps, then walk a few steps. Together.

Breathe in, sing out—yes, sometimes all we could do in our pain was sing, a hard-fought song of freedom. I looked from side to side. I looked ahead of me and behind me. My tribe never left. Deep gratitude washed over me for all of them and for this journey. And then I took my eyes off the tribe of supporters keeping pace with me, and there it was: the finish line.

"Let's pick up the speed, guys! We're almost there!" I cried out, my heart soaring with anticipation for a celebration so close I could taste it.

In that final stretch, I sprinted down the lit-up Vegas strip as if lives depended on it. I crossed the finish line, sweat pouring down my face and body, bawling rivers of tears. I couldn't believe I had made it. I didn't know what overwhelmed me most in that moment: that an amazing team of people had run this thirteen-mile race with me down the strip or that this same team had been running with me in the race of my life for the past year and would continue to do so.

At the realization that I'd made it, I collapsed a few feet from the finish line. Every muscle in my body was sore. Every dark corner of my past was conquered. I'd not only finished the race in Vegas, but I had now reached a milestone in my journey to graduation from the program.

I returned to my home in Kentucky to plan my graduation party. When the time came to celebrate together, the house was filled with people who all had some part in helping transform my life. My tears flowed unashamed and unabated. I proclaimed to everyone at this party exactly what I'd said after finishing the half-marathon. "I am exhausted. That was one heck of a race."

If I could pick a verse to sum up the year I spent facing every bit of my hurt and becoming ready to live life in my newfound freedom, it would be 2 Timothy 4:7: "I have fought the good fight, I have finished the race, I have kept the faith." I can claim this verse for my own story from a boundless well of gratitude and a deep sense of being loved.

When I think about how I want my life to be remembered, I hope that these very words come to people's minds. I want people to think not of how far I had fallen, but of how far faith has carried me.

CHAPTER TWENTY

PURPOSE

AFTER MY GRADUATION celebration, I was now faced with a new task. As much as I loved my forever Refuge family, I knew I couldn't rely solely on their support. I needed to spread my wings and build a solid community for myself. I had decided to stay in Kentucky and make it my home, so it was time for me to put down roots, the kind that looked like spiritual friendships lasting for eternity. I wanted to create roots in my faith and a life grounded in love. (See Ephesians 3:17.) So I got plugged in at church and began serving in hospitality and recovery ministries. I joined Bible Study Fellowship, which allowed me to get to know God apart from religion and denominations. It was the first place I had ever felt like just me: a woman of God, eager to know and display his love. I continued to surround myself with people who were focused on him.

After a few months of reveling in my freedom, I felt led to spend time serving in the very ministry that had helped save my life. It was my way of offering a passionate "thank you" for what had been poured into me. I raised funds to help support myself as a missionary with the ministry, and I was thrilled to see all the support that came in for me to focus on serving. People from all over believed in the work God had done in me and would do through me.

I spent nine months making myself available to serve the ministry and the girls in the house. But during this time, my heart was breaking within me, and

I knew clearly it was time for me to leave. But I wasn't sure why. Logically, this was where God would use me. But the urge to leave was growing. Many times, I'd been told that God had plans for my life, and the last two years, I had felt like I was finally living out those plans. I'd brought comfort and awareness in churches, schools, and recovery centers through sharing my story. Now, I see that it was easy and only natural to mistake sharing my story for my purpose in life.

But at the time, when I began to step back and evaluate the new season God was preparing me for, I was still confused. I found myself sharing my own changing heart with Angie, who was a ministry volunteer, and another one of her friends. Her friend shared something with me that confirmed what one of my friends had recently said to me on my thirtieth birthday as she handed me the most beautiful Bible I had ever seen. (You know, the one you are certain you will store all your spiritual treasures in and pass on from generation to generation.) They both basically said to me, "Your testimony is not your purpose. It is just your testimony."

Now that two women I respected had spoken this over me, this truth began to sink in. And suddenly I understood. As the second year of my healing came to a close, I had to embrace the reality that it was time to live out my faith in the world. I decided the best gift I could give my sisters who were fighting for new life wasn't to be in the house with them. Rather, it was to live out the dreams God had given me. I was a new person with new aspirations, ready to discover life in its fullest.

Angie's friend went on to tell me that when I had shared how I was feeling at this crossroad in my life, she had seen a vision of me as a baby, and this reminded her that God had a unique purpose set apart for me when he created me. He had never wanted me to walk down those dark paths; I had made those choices. She was right! I was free now, free to pursue the very purpose for which I had been originally designed. While God is an amazing Father who works all things together for good, including my testimony, I understood now he also had other plans for me.

Someday I would again work in health and wellness to help others become and live as their most whole selves. Over time, God restored that vision in greater detail along with my original God-given desires. During my healing journey, that vision and those desires became God-centered. But even before the redemption for my health industry experiences unfolded, God began to plant a new dream in me. I realized that my whole life was a ministry, not just my past. So I would need more equipping and a deeper understanding of what I believed.

I realized that my whole life was a ministry, not just my past.

Most of my life up to this point had been all about what I could do to serve myself. My achievements were used to build up my ego and not to help others. But from now on, I wanted to live other-centered. I believed that God used ordinary people for extraordinary things, so I also knew he did not require me to earn a degree to release me to serve others. But I *had* always loved to learn. Though a degree might not be necessary, it sure would be fun to pursue. Maybe it could open new doors for my still-unfolding future.

So the first step I took into this new dream was to apply for a Master's program at Asbury Theological Seminary. Before, I'd had no idea I could go to school to study the Bible. But because I loved school and I loved BSF, I knew that combining academic learning and biblical study would be so exciting to me. Unfortunately, I needed more than just enthusiasm to be accepted into seminary. In fact, I learned that getting into a Master's program was no easy task, but I still believed God could open doors no man could shut.

The first obstacle for me was that the school where I had done my undergraduate studies in Holistic Health had shut down. I was four courses away from earning my B.A. when I learned this. Armed with the knowledge that I held less than the minimum credentials, I opened up conversation with Asbury anyway. And amazingly, God did pave the way before me. When I talked with the seminary, I was delighted to discover that they would transfer my community college credits to make up for what was missing from the now-closed university. I could take another class at a local university, and they would consider my application.

But then I had to take the GRE, and I scored 3 points lower than they required in verbal reasoning. I did have a satisfactory score on the analytical writing section, though, and since grad school consisted of writing a lot of papers, they noted this in my file. We then paused for about a year to consider if this was the right direction for me. During the waiting, my motivation began to wane. Sometimes when life gets hard and I face delays, I start to think that maybe what I'm waiting for is not God's will. But that's not what he teaches. He says to ask, seek, and knock. (See Matthew 7:7–8.) I was seeking and asking, but I had more doors to knock on before I threw in the towel.

As I prayed about what that next door might be, I focused on what was in front of me. I stayed plugged in to my support community and was working at a local gym and a tea room. I was living in the conviction that no day and no task was wasted when done in love. Speaker Bob Goff confirmed this truth when he came to tell of his adventures in love at my church. As I listened to him tell his story, I felt an instant connection with the experience he described. He shared how he sat outside the dean's office in law school and said, "You have the power to let me in. Just tell me to go get my books, and I will." Imagining him doing this lit a fire inside me—of delight, hope, and dedication. After hearing this story, I was all the more motivated to get into Asbury Theological Seminary. I was ready to knock on those doors.

About a year into the process, I pursued the life experience exception with Asbury, which would allow me to be accepted without a bachelor's degree. My advisor chuckled at this approach, since most people who applied for this exemption were not a mere thirty years of age. But then I began to tell them what it had taken for me to get here and how determined I was to use every bit of knowledge they would give me in service for the rest of my life. I had the faith, and I desired to grow deep in wisdom—for the sake of all those who I'd be able to serve on the rest of my journey.

Finally, in March 2014, I received my official acceptance letter to start school full-time in the fall. Even more amazingly, not only was I accepted, but I also received two scholarships. My dad, who's faith was deepening at the same time I was pursuing mine, choked up with tears as he continued to watch God's favor pour out in my life. My spiritual family rejoiced with me, too, and helped me move into my first dorm. God was truly giving me back years that I thought I had lost. Here was my redemption: I got to have a normal on-campus dorm experience like I'd always dreamed, at a school where I got to go solely because God told the administrators "Yes!"

I cannot begin to tell you all the life lessons I learned at Asbury about faith, friendships, love, and vocation. There, I met my husband—a man with his own faith and values, who never once ever pressured me to reconsider mine. I had learned that not every professing Christian man is truly a godly man, but this man was humble, teachable, kind, and considerate. Before dating, we were friends long enough that I could see that his character bore good fruit, and I knew his faith was sincere. We were from two opposite backgrounds but headed in the same direction: toward a life devoted to God and to a world in search of hope.

My education was never about me and what I could become; it was about getting closer to a God who wanted to be closer to his people.

My friends were right about my purpose. I now know that my primary purpose is to love God and love others. That has always been the point. Every assignment, task, job, and relationship is an outlet for me to do exactly that. My education was never about me and what I could become; it was about getting closer to a God who wanted to be closer to his people.

I continue to grow deeper in my understanding of grace so that whatever life brings me, I can extend the same grace that was granted me to others. The same grace that saved my life. I have tried every other avenue to happiness and peace, so trust me. Only one Man could grant me true freedom. I now look at my story and see that the grace of God, which came through Jesus, covered me from beginning to end. And the best part is, I haven't even reached the end yet. Grace is covering me as I keep dreaming, living, and running the race of faith. Grace is before me, behind me, and on every side as I continue to live the fullest life, the one only Jesus could give me.

Though my story is far from over, every book must come to an end. So let me leave you with this: freedom is not the right to make choices. Rather, freedom is the ability to make choices that keep us free. I have so much more to tell you about how my new-found freedom has radically changed relationships in all areas of my life: family, friendships, work, and marital. But it's time for me to stop telling my story so you can live yours. When he made the ultimate sacrifice, he had me and you in mind. Just like me, God included you, too. Even though he knew every turn you would take on the roads that you've walked, he said, "Yes. I pick *you*." God is able to do far more than you can think and imagine. (See Ephesians 3:20.) Will you let him?

Gratefully His,

Deanna Lynn

A THRIVING REFUGE FOR WOMEN GRADUATE

Endnotes

1 Bob Goff, *Love Does: Discover a Secretly Incredible Life in an Ordinary World* (Nashville: Thomas Nelson, 2012), 48.

2 Andy Stanley, "The Right Person Myth," YouTube, 51:28, December 20, 2017, https://www.youtube.com/watch?v=_RqbijonXGI.

EPILOGUE

GOD IS GOOD. God is so good that he not only made a difference in my life, but he continues to make a difference in the lives of those around me with his radical love. I wanted to add a chapter to this book with updates on the people I wrote about. No relationship is wasted, but some were harmful for me, and I could no longer remain in them. Still, I learned much from each one.

The first one is my mom. My mom was in a lot of pain. I am not sure of the origin of her pain. I wish I had more insight into her upbringing and the generational cycles that went before me so that I could better prepare my upcoming generations. I'd love to pray more intentionally for any living relatives I have. My mom died so young and is now free to be with our Jesus. She no longer has to strive for attention or affection; her daily love tank is full. While my relationship with my mom left pretty deep scars, I can say I notice a few qualities in myself that were gifts from her. For instance, I have a love for birds and all animals. My porch is decorated with feeders and houses for my new winged friends in the neighborhood. I have a huge heart for the vulnerable, which I saw in her. I am organized and work hard at any job or task I am given. I am intelligent and ambitious, and I complete tasks, thanks to her example and work ethic.

Next is my adopted dad. This man never walked away. Every woman in our family ran away from him at different times in our lives, but he never left us. Just like our faithful Father, his love was not dependent on who we were or what we did. His love was an example of who he was, and it was unconditional. His love came out in dysfunctional ways for a season as he tried moving on from his pain without surrendering it to God, but he stayed the course, which says a lot.

When he met the woman he married, they pursued God while they pursued a relationship with each other. That void he had growing up was filled. Though still a very capable man, he is now less reliant on himself and more reliant on

God. I am proud to call them both my parents. They continue to support me in my endeavors, such as marriage, ministry, and starting a family of my own. They take many vacations to enjoy the second chance God has given both of them.

My sister also works very hard, following the example set by our mother. She still suffers from the effects of the many painful experiences she has endured. She continues to search for lasting healing in her own life and encourages my growth as well. She and her husband have raised three amazing kids. Her family could use our prayers as she uncovers what God has in store for her and her family.

Dru sought healing in his life while I was seeking my healing. He caught glimpses of love and freedom and gained much support along the way. Everywhere Dru went, he attracted a wealth of love. People could not help but want to be near him, be like him, and want what was best for him. Together, Dru and I were not healthy, but separately, I could pray for him to have the greatest life God had in store for him. At times, I couldn't pray anymore, as it felt too intimate, so I reached out to trusted friends who prayed for him every day when I couldn't. Dru was baptized the Easter after I was. He found a group of supportive men to help him walk out his relationship with God. Unfortunately, he was still very sick physically due to his addiction to pain pills. He overdosed two Easters later. He is free from his pain now, but his loved ones still carry some of that sorrow, and we always will.

His life had so much purpose. Even today, people are seeking help because of the example he set in trying or because of the people they encountered at his funeral service. He was a natural-born leader; those skills had yet to be harnessed and set loose for eternal good. However, our God works all things together for good, and his leadership and healing efforts are saving the lives of many and pointing others to everlasting life. I believe this will continue until eternity. When one person's life is touched by love, it affects one more person, and the ripples cannot be counted because they are too great.

His brother-in-law and sister walked away from the porn companies Dru worked for, and they believed God enough to step fully into their new lives.

They lead Bible studies and host group dinners. They care for the children's ministries, and Keith is known as the beach evangelist. Check out his book, *Just Breathe*, in my list of resources. He starts recovery groups and is a walking witness for Christ. They have used their leadership and business skills to open up companies that give jobs to those in recovery, who are hoping to regain some dignity—the same dignity someone helped each one of us find in our own journeys. They may even open up a center in Dru's memory one day to continue to reach people who suffer from the bondage of addiction.

These are just a few updates. I could tell you one story after another of a person who has overcome their own nightmares through encountering the faithful love of Christ. I might write another book with those stories someday, but for now, you'll have to take my word for it. There is no telling what can happen when we believe God. When we believe God, we begin to take the necessary steps to get well. Sometimes this means going into the rooms of recovery and/ or seeking medical help and what's needed to heal our physical bodies. We can't love God or others here without our bodies. For some, this will mean living beyond that initial moment of salvation and into the whole life transformation God intends for each of us. God has a purpose for you now. There is freedom on the other side of pain. Allow him to transform it, to transform you. Kneel, sit, listen . . . what is your next step?

UNPACKING YOUR STORY

UNPACKING YOUR STORY: QUESTIONS FOR REFLECTION

If you relate to any parts of my story, I'd encourage you to pursue deeper levels of freedom, including talking with a trusted friend or even a professional.

Nowhere in the Bible does God cover up people's struggles and shortcomings. Instead, the narrative allows us to relate to humanity as a whole and uncover the love available to us when we allow ourselves to be fully known. You may not be able to relate to my story, but everyone has a story, filled with relationships that influenced their belief systems, filled with times they felt like throwing in the towel, choices they made to escape through achievement, food, and binge watching their favorite show. I can't tell you how beneficial it was for me to identify the key factors that shaped my thinking and who I was becoming. I encourage you to bring your story before God and someone else and discover where your story collides with the grand story of life.

Part I: Past

Family: Family can come in all shapes and sizes. I collected family along my journey: neighbors, church family, friends of my family members, and even my friends' family members. I eventually had enough pieces of a family to feel what it was like to have a whole family.

1. Do/did you know a healthy family that gives you a tangible idea of what healthy love looks like? What values do you see in them that help shape the future family you would like to have? Who is your future family made up of?

2. Was there ever a time in your life when you felt like running away from home? What made you come back?

3. Was there any dysfunction in your family that directly or indirectly influenced you? Have you ever been blamed for someone else's pain or poor choices? How did that make you feel about yourself? What is the truth of that situation?

4. Were there any secrets in your home that no one was allowed to talk about?

5. Even in the most dysfunctional family, we can take away something good. What are some of the values or lessons that came from your upbringing that helped shape who you are today?

Friendships: I once heard that you are the average of your five closest friends. If this is true, it's important to evaluate who is in your inner circle and what imprint they are leaving in your life.

1. What kind of people did you surround yourself with growing up?

2. How did they influence your faith and life?

3. What kind of friend were you to others?

4. What are some weaknesses in you that can hurt a good friendship?

5. What valuable gifts do you bring to the table in your friendships?

Part II: Present

Faith: This is a deeply personal journey that no one can force on you. Our God promises that if you seek him with all your heart, you will find him. He did that for me. In my faith journey, I discovered a lot of bad things happen in this world because people put themselves above God. This was not his will or plan, but we are not alone in suffering. God is not afraid of our doubts and emotions. He meets us there if we allow him to. He will give us glimpses of his original design and our future life.

1.   Who do you put your hope in?

2.   Where in your life have you seen God at work?

3.   Who in your life influenced your faith in either direction?

4.   Who in your life can you now ask questions about your faith?

Freedom: As you read, it was easy for me to hide behind mask after mask out of fear that others would not love me for me. I hid behind addictions, accomplishments, people, and an entire new character all together! I can't tell you the weight that has been lifted off me since I don't have to protect myself but can find security in God.

1.   What does it mean for you to feel secure?

2.   In what ways do you try to secure and protect yourself that may instead be preventing you from the freedom you desire?

3.   What would it take for you to feel comfortable in your own skin?

4.   Who in your life accepts you as you are but loves you too much to allow you to stay there?

Part III: Future

Romance: Andy Stanley says we ought to become the person that the person we are looking for is looking for. After learning to be a good friend, what does that mean for us as we navigate the world of dating?

1.   Who were/are you looking for?

2.   What characteristics are you attracted to?

3.   Are you currently living in such a way that this type of person would be looking for you too?

4.   In the future, you might decide one day to pursue intimacy in the form of marriage. What areas in your life need improvement in order to benefit your current or future spouse?

5.   What does the word intimacy mean to you?

Sex: Sex is a great gift when it's the culmination of all other areas of intimacy you have with your spouse. Within covenant relationship, sex brings a blessing, security, and freedom to explore one another, body and soul, for as long as you both shall live. However, when sex is your sole source of connecting before ever achieving covenant oneness with your mate, it can be devastating to you, the other person, and your future spouses if left unhealed.

1. When were you first introduced to sex and how?

2. What or who else has influenced your beliefs about sex?

3. Are there any myths that you need to lay down in this area to come to a healthy, realistic view of sex?

4. What role does sex play in your design for intimacy?

Identity: The things we go through, the roles we play, and the struggles we have do not define us. Instead, they offer us a unique perspective. Each part of our personality and makeup give us a unique way of seeing and experiencing the world. It's not about what we've done but who we've become.

1. Who do you want to become?

2. What decisions are currently hindering you from becoming that person?

3. What decisions are helping you to become that person?

4. Who can you reach out to, to help you to become that person?

5. What is God's role in empowering you to become that person?

Dreams: For a dream to come true, you must begin with a dream! Sometimes those dreams are sidetracked by our own choices or choices that were made for us before we could choose what direction our life should go. It's time to discover your dreams.

1. What did you dream of when you were a little girl?

2. What new dreams do you hope to achieve once you have taken the time to grieve any lost or delayed dreams?

3. One wise decision leads to another. What step is in front of you today to pursue your new life?

As we mature, we will navigate new relationships, roads, and roles. It's okay if your dreams go a different direction as you become a different or more whole version of yourself. That's all part of growing into who you are! I encourage you to show up to life today and surround yourself with people who will help you do that. I look forward to hearing more about who you are becoming.

RESOURCES

Healing did not happen overnight for me. This process required community and resources that helped me to get to the truth. Here are some books and groups to help process and encourage growth.

Books:

Christian Codependence Recovery Workbook by Stephanie Tucker

Embracing Brokenness by Alan Nelson

Every Woman's Battle by Shannon Ethridge

Healing the Wounds of Sexual Addiction by Mark Laaser

Just Breathe by Keith Repult

Lord, Heal My Hurts by Kay Arthur

Reasons to Live: One More Day, Every Day by Jas Rawlinson

The Meaning of Marriage by Tim Keller

The Purpose Driven Life by Rick Warren

The Story of God, the Story of Us by Sean Gladding

Scars and Stilettos by Harmony Dust

Groups and Literature:

Adult Children of Alcoholics
and Dysfunctional Families: https://adultchildren.org

Alcoholics Anonymous: https://www.aa.org

Celebrate Recovery: https://www.celebraterecovery.com

Bible Study Fellowship: https://www.bsfinternational.org

Faithful and True–sexual addictions: https://faithfulandtrue.com

The Ultimate Journey: http://www.theultimatejourney.org

Made in the
USA
Lexington, KY